canine
communication

How to read your dog

Dr Justin Wimpole BVSc (hons) MACVSc
and **Dr Kate Patterson** BVSc (hons)

NEW
HOLLAND

First published in Australia in 2008 by
New Holland Publishers (Australia) Pty Ltd
Sydney • Auckland • London • Cape Town

www.newholland.com.au

1/66 Gibbes Street Chatswood NSW 2067 Australia
218 Lake Road Northcote Auckland New Zealand
86 Edgware Road London W2 2EA United Kingdom
80 McKenzie Street Cape Town 8001 South Africa

National Library of Australia Cataloguing-in-Publication Data:
Wimpole, Justin.
        Canine communication.

    ISBN 9781741105575 (pbk.).

    1. Dogs—Behaviour. 2. Dogs—Training. 3. Human-animal
    communication. I. Patterson, Kate. II. Title.

    636.70887

Publisher: Fiona Schultz
Managing Editor: Lliane Clarke
Project Editor: Michael McGrath
Editor: Kirsten Chapman
Designer: Natasha Hayles
Production: Linda Bottari
Printer: Publisher's Graphics, USA

Acknowledgements

Our families have been very supportive and we would like to thank Denis, Helena, Martin, Roger, Janice and Lisa. In our very busy lives our friends remain very important to us and we would also like to extend our gratitude to them. We work very closely with our colleagues who are a kind of family away from home. We thank them for their ongoing support.
A special thanks goes to our canine companion, Milo, and our feline friend, Beetle, who generously share their house with us.
We thank Fiona Schultz and the staff at New Holland and our agents Xavier Waterkeyn and Clare Calvert of Flying Pigs for their support.
Finally and most importantly, we would like to thank all of the animals that we have treated. Our patients continue to stimulate us and teach us new things every day.

Disclaimer

Dedication

For Zara and Dost

Contents

Introduction   6

One: Dogs are pack animals   10

Two: Normal canine behaviour and body language   20

Three: The early days   38

Four: Building a relationship with your dog   60

Five: Your actions influence your dog's behaviour   64

Six: Other animals influence your dog's behaviour   81

Seven: Illness can influence your dog's behaviour   86

Eight: Canine anxiety   91

Nine: Abnormal repetitive behaviour   108

Ten: Canine aggression   122

Eleven: Barking and vocalising   157

Twelve: Digging, destruction and other common canine conundrums   164

Index   182

Introduction

Canine companions play a central role in our lives today and have had a fundamental relationship with people throughout history. As veterinarians, we have dedicated our lives to helping animals, most specifically dogs and cats.

Justin's previous books, *First Aid for Dogs* and *First Aid for Cats* were written for dog and cat lovers who wish to arm themselves with the tools to help their pets in an emergency. Unfortunately, many dogs are not so lucky.

In Australia hundreds of thousands of dogs are surrendered each year to animal refuges, pounds or veterinary hospitals, and, due to lack of resources, the majority of these are ultimately destroyed. The single biggest reason that the dogs are put down is not untreatable medical disease or irreparable injury, but behaviour problems. In America and Europe, where there are more owners, the number of dogs that are surrendered and destroyed is in the tens of millions.

Due to this massive, futile waste of canine lives, we decided that—in addition to saving sick or injured animals in our day-to-day work—we would direct our focus to helping healthy animals with undesirable behaviour characteristics. As veterinarians, we work with dogs every day, so it is crucial that we understand the best way to interact with them. One of our aims in writing

Canine Communication is to help you to better understand what your dog's behaviour is telling you, which will enrich your relationship with your dog. We hope that learning more about canine communication will also prevent behavioural problems developing or help you to correct them when they do occur. If this can be achieved, hopefully, fewer dogs will be surrendered.

Dogs have a long history of living with people in various settings. In the wild they are naturally pack animals. The hierarchical structure of the pack is very important and will be discussed in more detail in Chapter one. In domestic situations the people and other dogs in the family form the dog's pack. The way people relate to a dog dictates its position in the pack and, therefore, the way that it relates to people in turn. This also means that it is quite easy for owners inadvertently to create behaviour problems in their canine companions. The key point to understand is that our behaviour influences that of our dog.

Dogs do have an inherent demeanour and natural character traits. Some of these are related to the dog's genes, and there are traits that are more common in particular breeds—certain breeds have even developed a bad reputation. Some dogs are simply 'naughty' by nature. This does not mean that the dog's behaviour cannot be modified. It just means that it needs to be managed long term. It is possible to keep a 'naughty' dog if you are prepared to work with the dog for life. Genetics are only partly responsible; the way a dog is raised and looked after and the environment the dog lives in play a major role in determining the dog's demeanour. You need to understand why the dog behaves the way it does and how to communicate effectively in order to manage your dog's behaviour.

The important role that dogs play in our society and the close relationships they have with our families are fantastic. However, the contemporary culture of treating dogs like people trapped in canine bodies has the inevitable consequence of confusing dogs. It can put undue stress on the dog because it probably wants to be a dog, but constantly has to expend energy maintaining a person-like role.

We have written this book both as veterinarians and dog owners. We have our own pack consisting of a beautiful boxer dog, Milo, and a playful cat, named Beetle. We by no means always have perfect pack zen. A pack structure is a dynamic entity, and different issues invariably arise from time to time. As veterinarians we are lucky to have been trained to deal with these and to understand how Milo and Beetle communicate with each other and with us.

Canine behaviour is very complex and, at times, can lead to extremely serious issues. Problematic behaviour threatens relationships, the safety of people and ultimately the dog's well-being and life. No text can hope to give a dog owner a complete understanding of canine behaviour and all the skills required to solve every problem. There is rarely a quick fix and solutions usually require constant management. For these reasons it is vital that you consult with professionals regarding any behaviour problem with your dog, especially if it involves aggression. The first point of call should be your veterinarian, with whom you should have an ongoing relationship.

It is important to remember that some behaviour problems might have an underlying medical basis. It is, therefore, helpful to provide your veterinarian with a clear history of your dog's health and behaviour. Ideally, you could also provide them with a video of any problem habits. You may also need to seek the advice of a behaviourist for further guidance and advice.

Canine behaviour problems are common and can be serious. You should seek professional help in managing behaviour problems.

1:
Dogs are pack animals

It is well known that the common domestic dog, *Canis familiaris*, is a descendent of wild wolves. Dogs and wolves are naturally social animals, and in many ways their social structure and methods of communicating are similar to ours. This is one of the reasons why dogs have been such good companions of people throughout history.

Domestic dogs retain their pack instincts today. In the wild a wolf pack is made up of two to twelve individuals. Wild dogs in urban or rural situations tend to form slightly smaller packs. Regardless of the size of the group, however, wolves or dogs living together naturally develop a hierarchical structure. This provides social stability and actually helps to reduce aggression between individuals.

One of the main advantages of the pack structure is that it helps the dogs to work together and therefore improves hunting efficiency. In a domestic situation, the members of the family become a dog's pack. How you treat and communicate with your dog dictates where it will fit into the hierarchy. Obviously, where dogs live with people, it is appropriate that the people are dominant to the dog. This means that a dog should perceive all people, especially its owner or owners, to be of a higher rank.

Most dogs naturally defer to people, and training reinforces this respect. However, some naturally pushy or dominant dogs try to reverse these roles if they are given the chance. Some dogs simply never learn to defer to people, and this can be a serious problem. As mentioned previously, your dog's behaviour or actions are greatly influenced by how you interact with it. At times it may be quite easy to elevate your dog's rank inadvertently if your dog misinterprets your intentions and way of communicating. This can cause behaviour problems and unnecessary stress on your dog.

Puppies as young as five or six weeks old start to determine their positions in the pack through play fighting. Initially their ranks fluctuate, and an individual dog's social position can rise and fall day by day. Gradually individuals find their natural position, and the pack hierarchy begins to develop stability.

A higher-ranking dog is considered dominant to a more submissive or lower-ranking dog, also called a subordinate. It is important to realise that dominance just describes a behaviour trait and does not automatically imply aggression. However, dominant dogs can sometimes develop specific abnormal and undesirable behaviour, such as dominance aggression (see Dominance aggression on page 135). Normally, conflict between two dogs regarding rank does not involve aggression—the submissive dog generally backs down from the more dominant one. Conflict is more common between dogs of similar rank, because they are more likely to challenge each other and compete for a higher rank.

It is oversimplistic to think of the pack structure as a top dog—or alpha—with subordinate dogs of descending rank below it. Pack structure is dynamic. A dog's position in the pack can change over time, or in different situations.

For example, a dog may be very confident and dominant in its own home or a park that it regularly visits and considers as part of its territory. This same dog may be far more submissive or of lower rank in less familiar surroundings, such as another dog's house or at the veterinary clinic. Dogs also form alliances, so one dog may also feel superior when another particular dog or person is around. The dog may naturally be very submissive or low ranking, but when its owner is walking it on a lead, for example, it may feel supported and more confident. The dog may be more inclined to challenge other dogs or people than it would if it was alone. This fluidity of the canine hierarchical structure is similar to our social structure, where a person's perceived position can change in different settings and as they mature.

Some dogs may be more likely to challenge another dog or person over certain issues, but remain very submissive over others. For example, food may be very important for a particular dog, and it may protect the food fiercely, even to the point of developing food-related aggression (see Food-related aggression on page 135). The same dog may be a pushover when it comes to other issues such as toys or sleeping location. The reason why certain things are more important than others is related to the dog's natural demeanour. The dog's individual preference influences the likelihood of conflicts and their outcomes and this is known as the game theory.

There are many circumstances in which a wolf or dog's rank might change over time, including when the dog is growing. As it reaches physical and social maturity, a dog develops new strength and confidence. Such a dog's rank may be elevated when a previously more dominant individual becomes elderly, sick or weak. Conflict is most likely to occur in these situations when the rank of each dog becomes closer (see Changes in rank diagram page 14). Ultimately, the conflict will be resolved and the individuals will settle back into the pack, possibly in an altered rank. If two individuals remain closely ranked, this may be a constant source of conflict.

The situation is similar for domestic dogs and can affect the relationship with both people and other canine members of the pack. It is important to understand these concepts in order to identify, understand and ultimately correct behavioural problems such as general defiance of an owner's commands and serious canine behaviour problems such as aggression (see Chapter ten).

> Conflict between a dog and other dogs or people within the pack, is more likely to occur when the ranks of the two individuals in the pack are very close.

Certain types of behaviour and physical characteristics determine which individuals are more dominant and therefore their rank. These traits and actions are outlined in Chapter two. The alpha or dominant dog may have several advantages, including access to the best food, the best place to sleep and the opportunity to breed with the best mate in order to pass on its genes to the next generation. The disadvantage of being the alpha dog is that it is more stressful— the dog constantly has to defend its position, and this uses energy.

Some dogs are just not cut out to be dominant or high-ranking dogs. It is unnatural and too taxing for them. Sometimes dog owners inadvertently elevate such dogs to an alpha position through constant doting. Many dedicated and well-meaning dog lovers like to see themselves and their dogs as equals. They share food with their dog, share their bed with their dog and they rarely discipline their dog. If their dog has a dominant nature, it will quickly assume the position of alpha, which can lead to serious behaviour problems. If they have an easy-

Changes in rank

- Rank reduction program
- Desexing
- Becoming elderly
- Illness

Decreasing rank

Similar rank and possibility for conflict

Increasing rank

- Approaching social maturity
- Inadvertent rank elevation

Pack members of similar rank are more likely to have conflicts. This diagram depicts how changes to the relative rank of pack members may lead to conflict.

going, more submissive dog, this constant, unintentional elevation to the alpha position can cause undue anxiety for the dog that would be more comfortable in a subordinate position. If severe, this stress can even lead to physical illness.

Loving your dog does not mean that you cannot be dominant to it. Your dog will not love you any less because you are of superior rank. In all situations, the best thing that you can do for your dog is to be a leader, not just a friend.

The way you behave towards your dog influences its position in the pack. As we have discussed, this may inappropriately elevate your dog's rank, but you can also use knowledge of hierarchy and pack structure to lower your dog's rank gradually. This can help to reduce your dog's stress level and avoid conflict with you and other dogs in the pack. This is known as a *rank reduction program.*

Rank reduction program

Used appropriately, a rank reduction program is one of the most important tools in managing your pack and modifying your dog's behaviour. This not only includes situations where lowering your dog's rank relative to you or other people is of benefit, but also where lowering a dog's rank relative to another dog helps too.

A situation where your dog sees itself as superior to you or other people is always inappropriate and needs to be addressed. Usually it is a combination of factors that leads a dog to view itself as the more dominant member of the pack or as the pack leader. Your day-to-day actions may inadvertently elevate its rank, as well as inadequate or ineffective discipline. For example, feeding your dog before the family eats may make the dog feel superior, because it thinks it has been offered the first and best choice of food. Similarly, feeding your dog from the dinner table not only encourages begging, but makes the dog feel that it is of equal rank to the people it is eating with. Another simple action that can influence your dog's rank is walking through a doorway or gate. If you allow your dog to go through first, it may feel higher in rank. Also if you allow your dog to sleep on your bed, the dog feels that it is sleeping in the best location, which further elevates its rank.

Restoring the pecking order, so that the dog's rank is below the other people in the pack, inevitably leads to the dog being more content and happier. The dog will please its owners more, rather than constantly being in conflict with or being chastised by them. Dogs really just want to fit in and please their owner, so this scenario tends to support a better relationship between you and your dog. If you have a multi-dog household, the use of a rank reduction program can also help you to reduce any conflict between them.

In the wild a dog may challenge another in order to reduce its rank, which may result in a fight. The outcome will determine each of the dogs' new ranks relative to each other. Obviously it is not an option for owners to challenge or fight their dog in this way to reduce its rank because this could be very dangerous. A much safer and more appropriate approach is to change some day-to-day factors to reduce your dog's rank gradually. This approach takes time and requires patience and perseverance, but is safer and more effective than a direct challenge.

It is important to involve all members of the family in a rank reduction program so that the dog's rank is reduced relative to every person. Children need to be involved, but should be supervised to ensure that they are being safe around the dog and are not inadvertently encouraging bad behaviour.

One of the most important principles is that dogs should earn everything they want by behaving well. For example, rather than just providing food, attention and affection at your dog's every command, you need to be the leader and dictate when your dog receives each of these things. To do this you need to teach your dog how to sit and wait in a calm and relaxed manner—on your command. In addition to the rank reduction program, these basic training skills are the greatest tools you can have to help to modify your dog's behaviour (see Basic training techniques, page 51). Sitting and waiting are submissive behaviours that you can use to ensure that your dog is deferring to you for everything. This will help to re-establish you as the alpha.

In a rank reduction program a dominant dog should be asked to sit and wait in a calm and relaxed way for everything. This means it needs to sit before it is fed, given treats, affection, toys or games or is allowed to go through a doorway, go outside or come back inside. This will reinforce to the dog that people are in charge and that it needs to obey and defer to them. If you give your dog a treat *before* it does something you ask—such as lie down in its bed—this is a bribe, and the dog has received the treat on its own terms. If you give your dog a treat *after* it does what you asked, then the treat is a reward, which has been earned and was given on your terms.

When you are training your dog, consistency is vital. You need to be vigilant 100 per cent of the time to maintain a more dominant position and ensure that your dog always perceives you as its leader. This can be very difficult, because some dogs are very subtle at controlling certain situations.

Some dogs may demand attention, for example. Giving your dog attention unconditionally may come naturally, but pushy dogs will take advantage of this. If you are preoccupied with work, reading or watching television and your dog puts its head in your lap, you may simply pat it. By doing this you have submitted to its request and given it attention on its terms. A simple action, which came so naturally and to which you hardly gave a thought, inadvertently lowers your rank as perceived by your dog. Although it may be difficult, a better approach would be to ignore your dog's advances initially, make it sit and, once it has obeyed, praise and pat it. This means that the dog has earned this affection from its leader and you have given it attention and affection on your terms.

Other more subtle actions can influence your dog's rank. If you are trying to reduce your dog's status or trying to maintain your superior position, you should not let your dog go through doorways or gates first. Ideally, you should make the dog sit and wait in a calm and relaxed way, then go through the doorway yourself first. Initially you may need to attach a light lead to your dog at all times so you can gently hold the dog back and ask it to wait as you step through the doorway. Then call it through and praise it for waiting, to reinforce the good behaviour. If you are trying to reduce the rank of one particular dog in relation to another, make the higher-ranking dog go through the doorway first. Then call the second dog through and praise both dogs for the good behaviour.

You can also influence your dog's rank by altering its feeding time. You should not feed your dog before the rest of the family. Make it wait until the family has finished, then you can feed it. Make sure you feed the dog away from the dining table or family eating area.

As previously mentioned, allowing your dog to sleep on your bed or on the couch may cause problems, especially if your dog has a dominant nature. For many people, letting the dog on the bed or couch is not a problem. Over time, however, it may contribute to the dog's perception of its elevated rank.

If you are having trouble moving your dog off the bed or couch, especially if it becomes aggressive when you try (see Chapter ten), you can use a long lead to gently pull it off. If you are not too close to your dog physically, it will not associate this removal from the couch with you. You should always pull the dog off carefully; never yank it off too quickly or forcefully, especially if it has had any injuries or history of neck or back problems.

As previously mentioned, a rank reduction program should be introduced gradually so as not to be too confrontational. For example, you should start with simple things like walking through doorways first and feeding the dog after the family has eaten. Once these activities become routine, you can move to potentially more confrontational interactions such as removing the dog from the couch.

Another very important tool in reducing a dog's rank is to neuter it, which is also called desexing. This applies to both male and female dogs, but is especially beneficial for dominant male dogs. This can be done either surgically or chemically. Each of these options has advantages and disadvantages, and you should discuss these with your veterinarian.

One of the main advantages of surgical desexing is that it is permanent. Chemical desexing can be used as a trial, to see how it will affect your dog's behaviour and how it will help the problem before committing to surgery, but it is only a temporary measure. Desexing your dog will not always eliminate the behaviour problem completely, but it usually helps. While hormones influence a lot of behaviour, much of it is learned and will not significantly change after desexing without using other behaviour-modifying techniques.

Rank reduction programs are integral in improving many canine behaviour problems, especially dominance aggression directed towards people or other dogs.

2:
Normal canine behaviour and body language

Dogs communicate with other dogs and people in several ways. They mainly use visual communication, which can be influenced by a large number of factors. Dogs also employ vocalisation, hearing, smell and touch to communicate. People also use multiple forms of communication, and the majority of these are also non-verbal— perhaps this is another reason why dogs have such a long history of living in harmony with people.

Despite these similarities, dogs are still dogs. Regardless of how person-like a dog may appear, dogs always stick to the natural methods of canine communication. Many people believe that their dog can almost talk. In reality, what people interpret their dogs to be saying is actually often inaccurate and can lead to a lot of misunderstanding.

One of the biggest mistakes people make is that their dog's signals or responses are equivalent to a person's. Although this is sometimes the case, most often this assumption is completely untrue. For example, many people think that when a dog licks them it is giving them a kiss. Canine licking is not the equivalent of a person's kiss and can have a variety of meanings. Kissing can actually be a behaviour used by pushy dogs to challenge or show dominance to other dogs or people. This is especially true when the licking is all over the person's mouth and face. By happily accepting licks all over your face, you may be unknowingly encouraging your dog's dominant behaviour and, in your dog's eyes, lowering your rank in the pack structure by deferring to the dog. Inadvertently encouraging such behaviour can lead to behaviour problems such as dominance aggression. Dogs may also lick to beg for attention or food. Remember, licking is a normal canine behaviour and it is important that you understand why dogs lick in various situations so you don't unwittingly accept unwanted behaviour.

Dogs have only a limited ability to learn our language, so, in order to communicate, we have to adapt to theirs. To speak to and understand your dog, you have to treat it like a dog and think like a dog yourself.

One of the major methods of canine communication is the use of visual signals and cues. Dogs start to develop their sense of vision as soon as they open their eyes, at about two to three weeks of age. They have relatively good eyesight and constantly use this to interpret signals from the environment. Compared to cats and humans, however, dogs actually have poor binocular vision (perception of depth). They do have excellent peripheral vision (out of the corner of the eye), which helps them to pick up visual communication signals. Dogs can see better at night than people, but their perception of colour is limited.

Most visual canine communication is expressed over a short distance, while other forms, such as vocalisation, play more of a role over a longer distance. Scent is also involved in long-distance communication and, of course, persists when more immediate visual and vocal cues have gone. Visual communication is often combined with tactile interaction (touch) to gain more information.

The major way that dogs send out visual cues is through the appearance of their body outline. Dogs can change the position of their ears, mouth and tail in order to do this. They can also alter their stance and are able to erect the hair along their back in order to convey a certain message. Various combinations of these signals convey different messages (see picture opposite). The shape, colour and markings of your dog can alter the signals it displays and, therefore, affect its ability to communicate accurately (see Your dog's breed affects the way it communicates: page 35).

Visual signs are also the main way that you, as an owner, can communicate with your dog. This is why you should gain some idea of canine body language. When a dog has aggressive intentions, it will tend to change its posture to increase its body size. When dogs wish to present an aggressive display or are frightened, they often also erect the hairs along their back and tail to increase their apparent size. In contrast, when it intends a friendly advance, it will change its posture to reduce its size, which will make its approach less challenging to another dog. More fearful or submissive dogs display such signs more readily.

The way a dog stands and the outline of its body can convey a lot about its demeanour. If a dog is very confident, it will stand tall, whereas if it feels more vulnerable, it will tend to have a more crouched stance. If the dog is being assertive, it will hold its neck outstretched and its head high. If it is being more submissive, it will tend to hold its head and neck low, and may weave and sway its head from side to side as it walks.

Another sign of submissive, non-threatening body language is an averted gaze, where a dog will not look directly at the other dog or person it is interacting with.

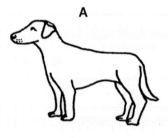

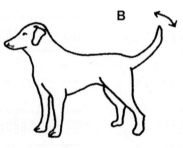

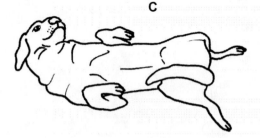

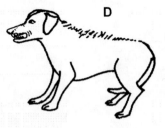

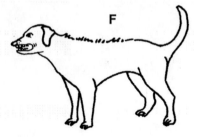

Dogs use their body position and tail to communicate.

A: *Relaxed dog.*

B: *Alert dog with an upright stance holding its tail high and wagging it with small excursions.*

C: *Submissive dog rolling on its back to expose its belly.*

D: *Fearfully aggressive dog with its tail between its legs and erect hair.*

E: *Submissive dog with a low, crouched stance and tail between its legs.*

F: *Assertive aggressive dog with tail held high and erect hair.*

A more assertive or dominant dog might make direct eye contact, which can be confrontational. Some very confident dogs might also occasionally avert their gaze as they approach another dog or person, but this is because they feel safe enough to look away. Challenging direct eye contact should not be confused with the intent stare of a dog that is actually looking up to a person or another dog with focus and admiration. Telling the difference will depend on the situation. For example, a dog that is keen to learn and follows your every move is more likely to have an admiration gaze, whereas a dominant dog may stare in a challenging way. More submissive dogs also tend to hold their ears down against their head. Erect ears indicate that a dog is listening intently in a confident manner.

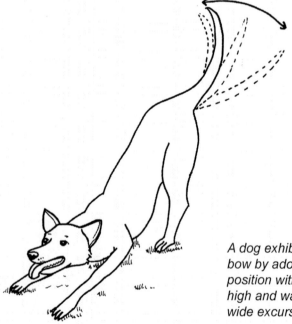

A dog exhibiting a play bow by adopting a praying position with its tail held high and wagging with wide excursions.

Tail position is important in canine communication. People commonly think that a dog is happy when it is wagging its tail. This is not always true, and, strictly speaking, dogs wag their tail only as an indication that they are prepared to interact. Depending on the other signals that the dog is sending, this may be a friendly interaction or a more assertive interaction. When a dog is being playful and is trying to encourage other dogs or people to join in, it generally holds its tail low, below horizontal, and moves the tail in a relaxed manner with broad movements. It may also exhibit a 'play bow', in which the front half of the body drops and the front paws are outstretched while the hindquarters are kept raised. During this the dog will generally wag its tail in a friendly way (picture opposite). A dog may also hold up a forepaw seeking attention, and this is a friendly gesture.

Generally if a dog is more confident or is being aggressive or wary, it holds its tail stiff and high above horizontal, and may wag only the tip. Just because a dog is wagging its tail does not mean that it is not being aggressive. Sometimes a dog displays mixed signals. For example, it may have its ears erect and be snarling with its teeth exposed, but it may still be wagging its tail. In this instance it is safest to take notice of the more aggressive signals and generally these are the facial expressions. As a dog displays more and more submissive, fearful or less confident behaviour, it will lower its tail below horizontal and even hold it between its hind limbs.

The position of a dog's mouth can also convey its intentions. If the lips are relaxed and loose, this suggests that the dog is also relaxed and passive. In comparison, tense, drawn-back lips that expose the teeth usually indicate an aggressive advance. Snapping jaws and growling indicate increasing aggression. It is important to note that some dogs play in a rough but friendly

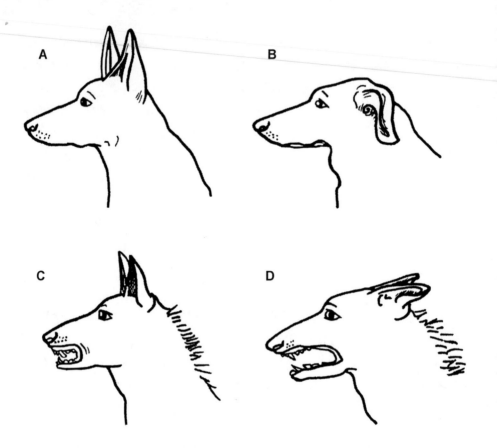

A dog's facial expression can indicate a lot about its frame of mind and intentions.

A: *A relaxed dog.*
B: *A fearful, submissive dog with its ears back.*
C: *An assertive, aggressive dog with its ears erect and snarling with lips raised and teeth exposed.*
D: *A fearfully aggressive dog with its ears back and snarling with lips raised and teeth exposed.*

manner and often growl and mouth each other around the face and neck. You can often determine if this 'rough-housing' is aggresive or not, because a playful dog will tend hold its mouth wide open and display other indicators of a friendly encounter.

> Caution: just because a dog's tail is wagging does not mean that the dog is being friendly.

Obviously if a dog is visually impaired, its ability to communicate visually is also impaired. Irrespective of age, it will not be able to receive visual signals from people or other dogs as accurately. If the dog has been visually impaired since birth, it will not be able to learn how to display these cues effectively. Visually impaired dogs will rely more heavily on their other senses, such as hearing, scent and touch. For example, a visually impaired dog will learn how to navigate its way around the house by touch and find out where things are by bumping into them. Once it has memorised the layout, such a dog can negotiate the furniture and other obstacles amazingly well.

Be careful when approaching a visually impaired dog, because it can be startled if you catch it unawares. To help to avoid this, talk to it before touching it. When you are happy that the dog knows you are there, you can allow it to smell you and you can touch it in a non-threatening way, such as rubbing it under the chin or on the front of its chest. Coming from above and patting the dog on top of the head is more threatening.

Another very submissive behaviour is for a dog to drop and roll onto its side or back, exposing its neck and abdomen for another dog to sniff. People often interpret a dog that presents its abdomen for a belly rub as being a happy dog. This is usually true, because if a dog is submitting to you, it is generally happy and relaxed and knows its place in the pack. If its tail is tucked during this visual display, then the dog is not only deferring to the other dog or person, but it is also frightened. If the dog also urinates, it is extremely timid and fearful.

Puppies commonly roll onto their side or back during play. This posture is different to the typical submissive posture, in that it is not completely passive and the puppy may use its forelegs, hind legs or both to push the other puppies away playfully.

In contrast to these submissive postures, some more assertive dogs execute different body language. For example, an assertive dog might approach another dog from the side and stand in a confident manner, with its head and neck over the other dog's shoulder. Another dominant or challenging move is for a dog to strike another dog's shoulder with its paw or place its paw on the other dog's shoulder.

The actions of one dog are influenced by its inherent nature, the particular situation and how another dog or person behaves towards it.

Mounting is normal canine behaviour that dogs, especially males, engage in from a very young age (see Mounting on page 178). Puppies often mount each other when they play. Mounting can be embarrassing behaviour for the dog's owner. Male dogs will mount both male and female dogs, and many people think that the behaviour is only sexual. In fact, most mounting is not sexual and has a role in determining social status, with more dominant dogs tending to mount lower-ranking dogs. The urge for a dog to mount is largely influenced by testosterone. However, some female dogs also mount. Male dogs that have been castrated, especially if this is done earlier in life, tend to mount less. Urine marking and leg lifting are also influenced by testosterone and castrated dogs will tend to do this less, especially if castrated early in life.

If a dog is approached by another dog in an assertive manner, it has several options of how it will respond, depending on its nature, how that relates to the other dog's nature and also on the situation. If the dog feels of similar or higher rank to the aggressively approaching dog, it may rise to the challenge and mount an assertive counter-response. Conversely, if the dog's rank is lower, it may respond with meeker, more defensive behaviour.

Defensive behaviour can be passive, and the lower-ranking dog may completely and unconditionally submit to the more dominant dog, perhaps by allowing the more dominant dog to put a paw on its shoulder or by rolling over to expose its belly. Alternatively, defensive behaviour can be more active, where the more submissive dog initially tolerates the superior-ranking dog, but if it pushes things too far, then the lower-ranking dog will retaliate with aggression as a last resort. When exhibiting actively defensive behaviour, a dog may snarl, bare all of its teeth and have the hair along its back erect, but it might have its head turned away from the more aggressive dog and listen for communicative

Examples of how dogs interact with each other.

A: *An assertive dog dominantly placing its chin on a more submissive dog's shoulder. Note the more submissive dog's averted gaze.*

B: *An assertive dog dominantly placing its paw on a more submissive dog's shoulder.*

C: *A submissive dog rolling on its back exposing its belly, actively submitting to a more dominant dog.*

A

B

C

signals with its ears. It will avoid direct eye contact, but will look at the superior-ranking dog from the corner of its eye and listen carefully to check for any aggressive advances.

Dogs communicate with people in similar ways to which they communicate with each other. This is important in your day-to-day interactions with your dog—and other dogs—and will help with training, recognising and correcting behaviour problems and, most importantly, recognising when a dog is giving you warning signs and may become aggressive. For example, if you are approaching a dog which is obviously fearful, you should squat down so that you appear smaller and less threatening. This is especially important if the fearful dog is showing signs of aggression, because if you are inadvertently too threatening, a fearful dog may attack. Similarly, if you suddenly approach a very dominant dog in an overly assertive fashion—making direct and unbroken eye contact or trying to pat the dog on the head or shoulder from above—the dog they may take this as a challenge and become aggressive (see Chapter ten). Instead, initially offer your hand under the dog's nose to smell, then you can pat it under its chin or on the front of its chest. Most dogs are naturally curious and will be interested to meet you. Make sure you watch the dog for changes to its body language that could indicate aggression.

Dogs have a good sense of hearing and can pick up vocal signals over a long distance. The sounds they communicate with include crying, whimpering, whining, howling, barking, growling, moaning and yelping. Crying, whimpering and whining are the first noises that puppies make, and dogs often continue to make these sounds into adult life. These may indicate that the dog is seeking care or attention or that it is begging from its mother or pack members. Similarly, dogs tend to howl to attract the attention of the pack, particularly if the pack is some distance away. This can become a problem with dogs that howl in the domestic situation to seek attention

Barking can be associated with aggressive behaviour, including claiming or marking territory. Often dogs bark simply to announce to everyone that they are present and to identify themselves. However, barking can become a nuisance if it is excessive or inappropriate.

Growling usually indicates aggression, and it may be accompanied by visual cues. It is commonly used for a short time as a warning, but can persist for longer if the warning is not taken and the situation progresses. Dogs might moan to exhibit enjoyment, such as when they are patted or are scratching. Yelping is a clear indicator of fear or pain, for example, if you accidentally step on a dog's toe or if it has an injury. If a dog associates a person with the source of pain, the dog may leap away and withdraw from that person. The dog might sometimes instinctively turn around and try to bite if it thinks that you are the one who hurt it.

You can use some basic aspects of canine vocalisation with your dog. If the way you deliver commands emulates the way dogs talk to each other, your dog is likely to learn these commands more easily, and you are more likely to have success. As a general rule, dogs use short, sharp sounds, such as short, repeated barks or whines, to ask their pack members to approach. So when you command your dog to 'Come', you should do so in a short, sharp manner with upward intonation. The actual command is less important and you can even simply use your dog's name. It is the delivery that is more important. Similarly, you can use longer sounds with steady intonation, such as 'Staaay' or 'Waaait', to calm and soothe or to stop a dog doing something. You can also use short, sharp sounds with a downward intonation as a command to stop a dog doing something such as 'No!', 'Ah!' or 'Bah!'

Dogs are very well known for their extraordinary sense of smell, and this is one of the major tools that they use to communicate. A dog's sense of smell is distinctly superior to a human's, so we cannot hope to communicate with dogs on their level. However, understanding how dogs use smell can help us to interpret their behaviour. Often, when dogs greet each other, they sniff each other's ears and groin area, which gives them various types of information about the individual they are meeting. Dogs also sniff people, presumably to learn a lot about them too.

Many dogs are particularly interested in smells while they are out walking. Dogs have several ways they deposit their individual scent as a marking, and other dogs can detect these in the environment. One of the ways a dog might leave its scent is by urine marking. This is why some dogs, especially male, seem to want to urinate on as many objects as they can.

Dogs also have two small scent glands near their anus called anal glands; when they pass stools, they usually release strong-smelling secretions from these. Dogs may also release anal sac secretions when they are nervous or frightened. Scents from the urine, stools, anal sacs and possibly from scent glands on their paws and other areas of their body might communicate information about the dog's territory, how long it has spent in a particular area or how often it goes there. Because dogs have a sense of smell that is so much better than ours, it is hard for us to understand this aspect of their world. For all you know, your dog may be having a distant affair with an unknown dog!

Urine marking and mounting are two behaviours that occur more commonly in male dogs that have not been castrated. Desexing or neutering may reduce these behaviours, but there is also a significant learnt or habitual component to them. This means that castration early in life may dramatically reduce a dog's tendency to urine mark, but might have less effect if done later in life. Castrating a socially mature male dog may have little or no effect on their urinary habits.

On the topic of urination, irrespective of whether a dog has been desexed or neutered or not, there is a huge range of normal urination postures for both male and female dogs. It is true that the classic cocked or raised-leg position is more common in male dogs. It is also true that the squat position is more common in female dogs. However, it is not abnormal for a male dog to urinate in a leaning position without raising his leg or for a female dog to raise her leg when she urinates.

Many owners of male dogs worry if their dog does not urinate in the typical cocked position, because they associate this position with maleness. However, a dog's preference to use the raised-leg position tends to develop more if it grows up around other dogs. It may not develop this preference if it was separated from its littermates while still quite young. Furthermore, male dogs are more likely to urinate in the cocked position if they are interacting with other male dogs or if they detect another male dog's urine or scent.

One of the basic needs of every dog is social interaction. The fact that scent is one of their main methods of communicating reinforces the point that dogs should not just be left to exercise themselves in their own yard, no matter how big the yard. They need to go out to deposit and receive smells, and this interaction occurs even if you don't see any other dogs on your walk. Some dogs might not like to pass stools in their own yard, presumably as they want to conserve this means of communication to use where other dogs will detect the scent. Some dogs scratch the ground after urinating or passing stools, and this action may emphasise the scent signal in several ways: other dogs and people may see them doing it; they will leave marks on the ground that could also act as visual cues; and they may deposit scents from their paws onto the ground.

Your dog's breed affects the way it communicates

Through intensive breeding programs over hundreds of years, people have created many very different breeds of dog, which are safe and suitable companions that can fulfill specific roles in society. An amazing feat of manipulation of the canine genome has produced tiny chihuahuas and tea cup terriers, which weigh less than 2 kilograms, and great danes and bull mastiffs, which exceed 80 kilograms. There are dachshunds with legs so short that their chests hardly clear the ground, while racing greyhounds have legs far longer than their wolf ancestors.

Some of the traits of modern breeds have greatly influenced their ability to communicate, usually by reducing it. For example a pug's nose is far shorter than a wolf's, and the lateral position of their bulging eyes compromises their binocular vision. In addition, domestic dogs may not be as good as wolves at hearing over long distances.

The most important features a dog can have to make its body language clear are pointy ears and a long tail. If the ears, lips and tail have a white tip, this can help to accentuate or highlight their message. Wolves and wild dogs tend to have these characteristics. Many modern breeds have been developed to exhibit features that are very different from their wild ancestors, with floppy ears, a short or tightly curled tail, a short nose and often few white markings. As a consequence these dogs are probably far poorer communicators. For example, whereas wolves have a long, pointed nose, breeds such as Shih Tzus, Boxers or Pugs have a shorter, more squashed nose. Possessing a shorter nose can inhibit a dog's ability to change its lip position as a form of communication.

Further adding to canine communication chaos are cosmetic ear-clipping and tail-docking—ear-clipping has long been illegal in Australia and tail-docking is now illegal in most of Australia. Another dog may not recognise a friendly advance in the park because the body language of the tail or ears of such dogs cannot readily be seen. The advance may be interpreted as being aggressive and so the other dog may respond in an aggressive way. Over time a dog that has been surgically altered may start to be wary of and even aggressive towards other dogs, because other dogs always seem to be aggressive to it. Some people believe that these misunderstandings have given docked breeds a bad reputation.

We own a boxer, named Milo, who, unfortunately, had his tail docked as a puppy before we adopted him. We believe he would be far better off if he still had his beautiful long tail. We are steadfastly against cosmetic tail-docking and ear-cropping. Taking away one of the dog's most important tools of communication may also reduce its ability to communicate with you and other people as well as other dogs. We liken it to cutting off your best friend's tongue.

In addition to these more general, imposed impairments, some breeds have more specific features that change their ability to communicate, at least with their canine compatriots. For example, a Rhodesian Ridgeback may appear to be in a constant state of arousal due to the raised ridge of hair along its back. Old English Sheepdogs and Pullis tend to have hair that covers their eyes, affecting their vision. This can make them less able to pick up visual cues from other dogs. In addition, the Pulli's dreadlock-type coat shrouds the silhouette of the body, obscuring the visual signals that they are displaying.

Such physical aberrations from wolves and wild dogs are not necessarily a reason to avoid a particular breed, but you should keep the canine methods of communication in mind when making your decision.

3:
The early days

Childhood is vital to a person's development, and experiences and influences during this time have consequences for the rest of a person's life. In the same way a puppy's upbringing can greatly influence its behaviour and relationships with other dogs and people.

Many things affect how a puppy develops. Some of these include: the puppy's breed, sex, whether or not it is desexed or neutered, the puppy's natural temperament, its training and its experiences with other dogs and people. You, as its owner and pack leader, can manipulate some of these factors, but a dog's inherent demeanour will also play a large role. If a dog has a difficult disposition, it can still be well behaved but might require constant management to achieve this. Some dog owners do not manage their dog in a careful way, such as the way we describe in this book. This is fine if the dog is easygoing, and many of these people are lucky and do not have a problem with their dog. However, behaviour problems are both common and serious, so it is important to take all precautions to prevent them developing. This is especially true if you have a pushy or dominant dog.

The right dog for you

Before choosing the type of dog you would like, the first questions to ask are: can I look after a dog, and is it right for me to buy a dog—or another dog? Owning a dog is a big commitment, in terms of finances, time and emotions. There are significant costs associated with owning a pet, with one of the most important being good-quality food. There are routine preventative health requirements for all dogs, including flea control, heartworm prevention, intestinal worm control and vaccinations. In addition there are the costs of veterinary care that may arise with any health issue. Although some breeds are more susceptible to certain medical conditions, any dog can contract any illness or become injured at any time. Pet insurance for your dog is a great idea, and is virtually essential, but is another ongoing cost to consider. There is also the cost of grooming, as well as day care and boarding when you go away. Transporting pets, especially internationally, can also be expensive. Most of these costs go up with the dog's size, another aspect to consider when choosing.

Dogs add so much to our lives and give back so much. However, they do also take up a significant amount of our time. The most important time commitment involved in owning a dog is providing it with adequate exercise. Every dog, except possibly the oldest or sickest, requires daily exercise. Without it, dogs lack mental and physical stimulation. This can lead to the misdirection of the excess energy and ultimately to serious problems like destructive or aggressive behaviour.

Inadequate exercise can also lead to canine obesity, which, as it is in people, is a very serious medical problem and can exacerbate many illnesses, with osteoarthritis probably being the most important and most common. The amount of exercise that a dog needs varies with breed, age and each individual.

In general, larger dogs tend to require more activity than smaller dogs, but many great danes, mastiffs or even retired racing greyhounds are happy to sit around the house and relax while fox terriers and jack russell terriers seem to have endless energy. As a consequence these dogs have a huge exercise requirement. Working dogs like border collies or gun dogs such as german shorthaired pointers, are likely to require much more exercise than toy breeds, which are happy with a more sedentary lifestyle.

Owning a dog is a big commitment and it is important that you choose the right dog for you.

Your lifestyle will dictate which breed is likely to be appropriate for you. Not only does a dog's breed influence how much exercise it needs, it also influences other things like grooming. Dogs with a long coat take longer to brush, bath and dry than short-coated breeds. Certain coat types, such as those on schnauzers, are more prone to gathering grass seeds than others. This might be important if grass seeds are common where you live, because they can sometimes migrate under the skin and cause problems. Of course, larger dogs take longer to groom than smaller dogs.

Certain breeds have other individual maintenance issues. For example, dogs that have many skin folds, like pugs and bulldogs, may require that you clean these hidden areas of skin regularly to prevent dermatitis. Pugs may also need to have their bulging eyes lubricated, while long-haired breeds, such as maltese terriers, may need the hair around their eyes trimmed and cleaned regularly to remove eye discharge, which can accumulate. Also, dogs prone to ear problems, like cocker spaniels, often need their ears cleaned regularly.

The size or strength of a particular dog can be an important factor to consider, and your choice will depend on you as an owner, your home and your lifestyle. An out-of-control, rambunctious newfoundland can easily drag an elderly lady into oncoming traffic, but this situation is much less likely to occur with a chihuahua! You should also consider the type of house you live in. Just because you may live in a small house or apartment, it does not mean you cannot keep a large or energetic dog. It just means that you will have to take the dog out regularly for exercise and mental stimulation. Having said that, you might not be too impressed by a saint bernard that constantly knocks vases and glasses from the table tops in your small apartment. On a similar note, having a large yard does not necessarily mean that you should choose a large or very active breed. Although many dogs exercise and amuse themselves to some degree within their own yard, they really require external stimulation from walks outside the yard, at places like parks or beaches. So whether or not you should have a large or active dog depends more on your ability and inclination to exercise it rather than how much land you have.

Something else to keep in mind when you are choosing a dog is that most breeds are predisposed to one medical condition or another. For example, Shar Peis can have skin problems, miniature schnauzers can have high blood fat levels and are at risk of pancreatitis, and cavalier king charles spaniels are at risk of heart valve disease and several neurological conditions.

When considering a particular breed, you should discuss any breed-specific issues with your veterinarian, other owners and breeders. Obviously breeders have a vested interest, so it is a good idea to also speak to unbiased sources. Some breed-specific health issues may not cause problems until late in the dog's life, so may not necessarily be a reason not to choose a particular breed.

Obviously temperament is another important factor to consider. Some breeds have a reputation for being very friendly, easygoing and good family pets, while other breeds are known for being aggressive. Although these reputations can sometimes hold true, individual dogs vary greatly. While cavalier king charles spaniels are very popular family pets and thought of as being very friendly and placid, the occasional individual may display severe aggression or other behaviour issues making them very difficult to deal with. Similarly american pit bull terriers have a reputation for being dangerous dogs, but some pit bulls are very placid and make great family pets.

Unfortunately, certain breeds have a bad reputation largely because of irresponsible owners who neglect their dogs or even by encouraging aggressive behaviour. Such treatment can cause some of the traits for which they have been bred, such as aggression, to manifest. Responsible breeders breed dogs with good temperaments.

Most dogs, irrespective of breed, can be fantastic pets if given adequate exercise, discipline and affection. Once you have chosen a suitable breed, it is important to talk to the breeder. Meet their breeding dogs and especially the parents of your puppy. Also talk to owners of other dogs from that breeder about the temperament of the dogs and any health issues that the dogs may have had. You should bear in mind that even taking all these factors into account cannot guarantee that an individual will have a particular temperament.

Every dog is unique. Some may be submissive, while others are more dominant and less easygoing. These dogs are more likely to push the boundaries of any discipline you impose. Easygoing dogs may seem better as family pets, but most dogs of various temperament types can potentially be suitable pets. What is important is that you properly train your dog, and that this training and discipline continues for the dog's life. Part of this includes being able to recognise signs of behaviour problems early and to seek professional assistance if required. This is especially important for dominant dogs, because these dogs can more easily develop extremely serious behaviour issues. It is important to understand that owning a dominant dog as a pet may not be a problem, but failing to manage it appropriately can be.

Many people acquire their pet as a puppy, usually from a breeder, rescue organisation or pet store. Obviously this means that the puppy is chosen well before it reaches social maturity, which occurs at about 18 to 24 months of age, but can occur slightly earlier or later. The true temperament of a dog may not be fully developed until the dog is mature, so it is very hard—if not impossible—to select a young puppy with a specific temperament type. Similarly, some behaviour problems may not manifest until the onset of social maturity. Sometimes first impressions can be misleading. For example, when you meet a litter of puppies, a particular puppy may seem very calm and quiet, but this may be simply be because it has been playing all morning and is exhausted. Similarly, if a puppy has been caged or has not had any attention prior to your visit, it may go berserk when it is first let out and appear hyperactive but may later settle down.

For this reason, it is important to spend sufficient time with a puppy, both alone and with its littermates, to help you to find out what it is like. Some puppies may be very shy and reclusive when they first meet their prospective owner, but may improve with time and subsequent meetings. If possible, you should arrange to visit the puppies on several different occasions, which will help you to understand each of the puppies better and give you a chance to think about this important decision.

It can be very helpful to ask the carer of the puppies about each of their temperaments, level of activity, daily routine, interaction with other puppies and progress with toilet training. Some people use temperament tests and puppy aptitude tests to help to determine a puppy's suitability. However, the results of these can be misleading, probably because they are performed on immature puppies. Ultimately, picking a puppy is a bit of a gamble, but, remember, dogs of all temperaments can potentially make good pets, some just need more management to help to prevent behaviour problems.

Sometimes it is not so much a case of you making the decision to buy a puppy, but a case of the puppy or dog finding you! This can happen if a stray dog comes into your life or if you acquire a dog from a friend who cannot look after it anymore.

Adopting a homeless dog is a wonderful thing to do, but there are some issues that you need to consider carefully. In this situation you have no choice in the dog's temperament, size, breed or its age. Can you have a dog at all and is that particular dog suitable for you?

If the dog is socially mature, you will have a more accurate idea of its temperament than if you chose a puppy from a litter. However, there is a risk that the dog may have already established behavioural or medical problems. Even if such problems are not immediately evident, you should be cautious: these are the two most common causes of dogs being abandoned. Such dogs' problems may require life-long management, so these dogs are best off with a loving and committed owner. An aggression problem is a very serious issue. Even if it is manageable, adopting such a dog may put you, your family and other dogs around it at risk until the problem can be controlled.

Aiming for a well-adjusted puppy

There are critical times for learning in the first few months of a puppy's life, known as developmental or sensitivity periods. It can be very important that puppies are exposed to certain things during these periods in order to become a well-adjusted dog. If a puppy misses out on these experiences, it is not doomed to develop behaviour problems, but the risk is increased.

Puppies learn how to interact with other dogs best when they are around three weeks to eight weeks of age, usually while they are still with their mother and littermates. This is an important time for them to learn essentially how to be dogs, and this is when they develop the concept of a pack. From as early as five weeks through to twelve weeks of age, puppies learn how to interact with people. From around ten weeks to sixteen weeks of age, puppies become very curious and are receptive to new environments and experiences. If a puppy is not exposed to other dogs or a variety of situations during the first four months of life, it is at risk of becoming fearful of new experiences as an adult dog and may develop abnormal responses to them. If a puppy does not interact with different people during this time, it may become shy and fearful of new people as an adult dog, which can lead to problems such as fear aggression (see page 128).

You should expose your puppy to other dogs and people of various ages and sexes to help it to acclimatise and to avoid inappropriate fears. Obviously you may be concerned about doing this with a puppy that has not yet received its full course of vaccinations. Many vaccination schedules are not complete until sixteen weeks of age. However, as long as your puppy is socialised with other healthy and, ideally, vaccinated dogs, the risk of contracting an infectious disease is low. Before the vaccination course is complete, though, it is probably not safe to take your puppy to the dog park, where you do not know if the other dogs have been vaccinated. The controlled environment of puppy school or socialising with a friend's dog you know is healthy and vaccinated is safer.

Withholding socialisation can cause the puppy to become fearful of other dogs, because it does not learn how to interpret canine language and so will not be able to interact with them appropriately. Problem behaviour is the biggest killer of dogs in our society, so denying your puppy these critical learning opportunities could potentially have devastating consequences. If you are concerned about the disease risks, discuss these and your puppy's vaccination status with your veterinarian.

The learning and developmental periods are also a great opportunity for puppies to grow accustomed to various stimuli such as cars and traffic, bicycles, vacuum cleaners, loud music, alarms, storms, fireworks and other animals that it will live with. If a puppy is going to spend time on a farm as an adult, it should be carefully exposed to farm animals. If it is going to go to a work place, it should also be exposed to this environment as a young dog. It is important that all new experiences are introduced slowly and that overall the experiences are positive. Check that the puppy does not show signs of distress, as this can also impair learning. Make new experiences fun, and reward your puppy with praise, pats and food treats when it reacts to the new experience in a positive way.

Your young puppy should have controlled exposure to various other dogs, people, environments and experiences. Make sure these are safe and pleasant.

Puppies need some exercise; the amount varies with its breed and generally increases as the puppy reaches maturity. Puppies need discipline so that they can learn which behaviours are acceptable and which are not. Setting boundaries helps to establish you as the clear leader of the pack. Establishing a routine early also helps the puppy's learning process. Just like children, puppies with regular meal times and exercise times are more likely to be well adjusted and relaxed. Puppies also need affection to help them to feel part of the pack and to develop a bond with their owner and other people. As the leader of the pack, you should teach your puppy good manners. From the outset teach your puppy to release its food and bowl to you at any time (see Food-related aggression on page 132).

Children cannot raise themselves and neither can puppies. Allowing a puppy essentially to raise itself in a yard and hoping that it will develop into an acceptable pet is unrealistic. It cannot be stimulated sufficiently and does not receive enough exercise. Nor will the puppy receive adequate discipline that teaches it how to be an acceptable pet, how to relate to people and possibly how to relate to other dogs. It will be deprived of the affection that helps it to learn and feel part of a pack. Without these basic elements, the dog will be forced to cope by entertaining itself and will learn its own set of rules. Some of these may be unacceptable and develop into serious problems such as destructive behaviour (see Destructive behaviour on page 164).

Raising a puppy is a big commitment. It requires additional dedication during the early periods of learning and development and also when the dog reaches social maturity, which is at around 18 to 24 months of age, but can occur slightly earlier or later. If you spend sufficient time interacting and training a puppy by providing exercise, discipline and affection, you will be rewarded with a well-behaved, well-adjusted and happier dog for life.

If, on the other hand, a dog is smothered with affection, but not given adequate mental stimulation, exercise and discipline, it will become spoilt and this can develop into defiance. Because each dog has its own specific character traits, some dogs will be more prone to developing certain behaviours. For example, very dominant dogs may develop dominance aggression in certain situations while very submissive dogs may develop fear aggression. Just like children, though, remember that dogs are individuals; how they turn out is not only due to your good work nor is it only your fault!

Basics of toilet training

One of the first challenges of training a puppy is housebreaking them. This is one aspect of learning that most owners are very motivated to achieve early. Prior to around seven to eight weeks, puppies go to the toilet pretty much indiscriminately, although they generally avoid it in their sleeping area. Once they reach seven to eight weeks, puppies start to become more choosy about where they toilet. It is normal for young puppies to urinate as often as hourly during the day and once or twice overnight. Puppies may pass stools around four times per day.

Toilet training should start from eight to nine weeks of age. The ideal way to train a puppy to urinate or pass stools in a specific location is to take it to that area regularly, especially after eating and immediately after waking up or play. Taking your puppy there often will give you the opportunity to praise it when it toilets in the right location.

When puppies are taken outside they will not toilet immediately. Instead they will sniff around and investigate the area first, and this is a normal part of a dog's routine. If you allow the puppy only five minutes before giving up when it does not urinate, it will invariably toilet on the floor as soon as it comes back inside. Instead give your puppy 15 to 30 minutes to explore the area and to go. If it toilets appropriately, praise the puppy and give it treats, ideally as soon as it squats or raises its leg to urinate. If it is acceptable for your dog to toilet on several different surfaces such as grass, trees, tiles or asphalt, then take your puppy to all these areas. Similarly, if you want your dog to toilet only in one particular area or on one particular surface, then always take it to this area or surface. If you cannot take your puppy out regularly, you should provide it with absorbent material on which to urinate and pass stools, because it will need to toilet between these trips.

If a puppy urinates inside, don't punish it verbally or physically, as this can cause the puppy to fear that area of the house or even you. If you catch your puppy in the act of urinating or passing a stool in the house, startle it just enough to distract it from what it is doing without causing fear. Immediately pick the puppy up and take it straight outside to give it an opportunity to toilet. Again if the puppy performs outside, you should praise and reward it.

You can also train your puppy to toilet on command rather than simply in a certain place. To do this you should regularly take them out. When they perform you should immediately give your toileting command then praise and reward them. Eventually the puppy will learn to toilet on command.

Decide on which toilet-training strategy you would like to use from a young age to avoid confusion. Toilet training does not require advanced training skills, but it does require patience, persistence and consistency on your part. The rewards of properly toilet training your puppy are obvious. If you are committed, most puppies are fully housebroken by six to nine months of age. Also the effort required to housebreak a puppy is far less than that required to manage or correct inappropriate toileting in an adult dog.

However, if an adult dog is not fully housebroken, do not despair. Although it may be harder and you may require more patience, you can still use similar methods to housebreak or toilet train your dog.

Sometimes puppies dribble urine involuntarily. If this persists despite appropriate toilet training, take your puppy to a veterinarian because infections and other urinary disorders could be causing the problem rather than a failure of the puppy to learn.

Basic training techniques

Training is a critical component of raising a well-adjusted puppy, and this should start at an early age. The intensity of training may reduce as your puppy develops into an adult, however, it should continue to some degree throughout the dog's whole life. Healthy puppies can learn commands and specific behaviours from a very young age. Many puppies can learn to sit on command by as young as seven weeks of age. Puppy class can be invaluable to your puppy's development, not only for obedience training, but also for learning to socialise with other puppies and people.

Arguably the most important command you can teach your puppy is to 'Come'. This may seem obvious, but you cannot hope to proceed to 'Sit' or 'Stay' commands if you cannot first gain the attention of your puppy. Most puppies naturally want to come to you because they are curious, because you are the leader of the pack and also because you may have food. Take advantage of every time your puppy approaches you of its own accord, and repeat both its name and the command 'Come' every few seconds as it approaches you. Make sure you praise it enthusiastically, and give it a food reward when it reaches you.

Start each training session by gaining your puppy's attention with the 'Come' command. Be careful not to use it when you call your puppy in order to punish it, as the puppy will associate 'Come' with a negative experience and will be less likely to obey next time. If you need to punish your puppy verbally, use a short sharp 'No!' Then call the puppy with the word 'Come'. Praise it and give it a food reward if it comes to you. This quickly stops the undesirable behaviour by distracting the puppy and making it perform an alternative and more appropriate behaviour.

Another simple but important command that you should teach your puppy is 'Sit'. This is a vital basis for further learning and for many problem behaviour management techniques. Asking a puppy to 'Sit' can distract it from inappropriate or unwanted behaviour, and sitting in a calm and relaxed way gives the puppy the opportunity to be praised and rewarded.

Rewards are the most effective tool for teaching your puppy what is good behaviour and what is not. Most puppies are responsive to food and learn very quickly when they are working for it. Using food helps to focus the puppy's short attention span, but if your puppy is not particularly driven by food, there are other ways of rewarding good behaviour. This might be by praising and patting the puppy or by giving it a toy to play with when it performs your command. For further information on rewards, see the Rewards schedule on page 71.

If you are using food as a reward, hold a treat out in front of the puppy so it can see it first. Ask the puppy to 'Sit', repeating the word every few seconds as you raise the reward up over the puppy's head. The puppy will usually start to arch its neck back to follow the treat and will then probably sit down. As soon as the puppy sits, praise it by saying 'Good dog!', and immediately give the puppy the treat and a pat. If the puppy is backing up rather than sitting, hold your other hand behind its bottom. As the puppy backs up, it will bump into this and sit down. Alternatively, another person could stand behind the puppy so that it backs up into their feet and legs then sits down. Avoid actively pushing down on your puppy's hindquarters to force it into the sitting position. This does not accelerate your puppy's learning and, if forceful and repetitive, could affect your puppy's hip development.

Repetition is the key to success and fairly quickly the puppy will associate the 'Sit' command with the action of sitting down and the immediate reward. As the puppy masters this command, you can start to give the food reward only some of the time, then eventually not at all. Continue to give the puppy verbal praise when it performs. As with many training techniques, it is easier to teach 'Sit' properly from a young age. It is never too late to teach an old dog new tricks, but learning occurs much more effectively in the first few months of life.

Initially teach your puppy to sit in a quiet, calm environment where there are no distractions. When your puppy has mastered this, it is time to increase the challenge. Continue to practise the command in the presence of minor distractions, such as background television noise or additional people. Over time your puppy will learn to focus on you and perform the command in order to receive the reward. Gradually introduce more and more distractions, such as other dogs, to make the training sessions more challenging. When your puppy can perform the sit command reliably in these conditions, take it outside where there are many more distractions. You will need to practise this basic training command often, and by gradually increasing the challenge, you should be able to make your puppy sit and be relaxed in any situation, including during fireworks, a storm and even in the presence of new dogs at the dog park.

Once your puppy has conquered 'Sit', you can start teaching the complementary 'Stay' command, another fundamental part of basic training. It can be harder and take longer for a puppy to learn 'Stay'. For this reason 'Stay' has to be taught gradually and takes more patience on your part. Some dogs are more comfortable and more likely to 'Stay' in the lying position rather than in the 'Sit' position, which is fine.

Once the puppy is sitting or lying still, say 'Staaay' and hold one hand out towards it like a stop sign. Then take a small step backwards away from the puppy, but keep your hand extended. Repeat the command 'Staaay', then quickly step forwards to the puppy and, if it stayed still, enthusiastically praise it with 'Good dog!' and a food reward. Repeat this sequence of events several times, but take a slightly larger step backwards each time your puppy performs the command correctly.

Gradually extend the distance that you walk away and the period that you make the puppy stay. Remember to praise the puppy enthusiastically when it stays for the required time period. Gradually you can work up to a point where you can ask your puppy to 'Stay' then turn your back and walk away. Don't talk to your puppy over your shoulder as you walk away, because this may confuse it. You can then use a command like an enthusiastic 'Okay!' or 'Free!' to release it from its 'Stay' position.

If the puppy stands up before you release it, start the process again. First command it to 'Sit', then reward it. Then command it to 'Staaay', pause for a few seconds, then release it and reward it with praise and a food treat. If you do not correct your puppy when it breaks from the stay position, it will not learn that it has to maintain this until you release it. It is important to be consistent and practise often.

As with teaching your puppy to 'Sit', gradually increase the number of distractions. Once your puppy can reliably perform the 'Stay' command in a quiet environment inside, challenge it by introducing noise or other distractions. Step by step you can practise the command in more and more challenging environments. If you can train your puppy to sit and stay in the face of various distractions, you have a much better chance of controlling any inappropriate behaviour that may develop.

As your puppy conquers these basics, you can start to teach it other important skills such as how to walk on a lead, fetch a ball and other tricks like shake hands or roll over. There are many books available that outline various techniques you can use. Puppy classes—and obedience classes for older dogs—provide a great environment for dogs to learn, practise and improve basic commands and more advanced tricks. They also provide good social interaction with other dogs and people. Training your puppy continues through puppyhood and into its adult life. Remember, it is never too late to start teaching your dog these vital skills.

Routine puppy health and maintenance

As well as acclimatising your puppy to other dogs, people and various environmental stimuli, it is important that your puppy becomes used to routine maintenance procedures, veterinary hospitals and veterinarians. Introducing your puppy to bathing, brushing, nail clipping and administering medication, of both oral and topical forms (applied directly to the skin) will teach it to accept such activities and will help to avoid any inappropriate fears of them.

When a dog is not scared of the veterinary hospital, veterinarians and the physical examination, it is easier to treat, and this can be very important if it suffers from a severe or chronic illness.

Generally young puppies have to visit the veterinarian several times for routine vaccinations, microchip identification and desexing. You can help to make these experiences fun and non-threatening by praising your puppy when it is calm and relaxed and giving it a food reward when it does not show signs of fear. In addition you can take your puppy to the veterinary hospital just to visit, perhaps only to be weighed and to interact with staff. Such visits mean that the puppy's experience of veterinary hospitals and veterinarians does not always involve potentially frightening examinations. If the hospital is too busy for a long visit, then even a quick walk through the waiting room is still helpful. Puppy classes are often held at veterinary hospitals, and this setting is very beneficial for making visits to the veterinarian fun and a natural occurrence in life.

While discussing visits to the veterinarians, it is appropriate to cover the procedure of desexing or neutering. Veterinarians hear numerous excuses for not desexing a dog. Unfortunately, large numbers of dogs are destroyed in developed countries each year simply because they are unwanted, which means that is in the interest of the dog population in general for pets to be desexed. There are also significant health and behavioural benefits for the individual dog, especially if this is performed prior to the onset of sexual maturity, at around six to twelve months of age. Desexing or neutering reduces, in some cases eliminates, the risk of developing several potentially life-threatening diseases, such as breast cancer, testicular cancer or infection of the uterus.

If you neuter your bitch prior to her first heat, at about six to twelve months of age, she is around twelve times less likely to contract mammary cancer later in life compared to an undesexed bitch. If she is allowed to have one heat only before being desexed, she is around three to four times less likely to contract mammary cancer, and after the second heat this benefit is virtually lost. Undesexed or entire bitches can also develop a serious life-threatening infection of their uterus shortly after their heat called pyometra. The best treatment for this condition is surgical removal of the ovaries and infected uterus, which can be expensive. Neutering your bitch prevents this from occurring.

Often owners of male dogs are reluctant to have their dog castrated, feeling that this somehow reduces their dog's male characteristics. This may be true to some degree, but these effects are generally over-exaggerated. As with female dogs, there are significant health benefits associated with neutering male dogs. It prevents them from developing a condition called benign prostatic hyperplasia, which is an enlargement of the prostate that can occur later in life. Non-castrated dogs are also at risk of developing infections of the prostate, such as prostatitis or prostatic abscesses, which can be life-threatening.

Some people believe that neutering will change their dog's energy levels, causing it to become less active and so overweight. However, diet and volume of food have a far greater bearing on a dog's weight than desexing, and as an owner you have ultimate control of what and how much you feed your dog.

Some people also think that desexing will change their dog's behaviour and natural demeanour. Dogs reach social maturity at around 18 to 24 months of age, but this can occur when the dog is slightly younger or older. As a dog grows, its demeanour naturally changes over time. However, this is not necessarily related to the desexing procedure. For example, there is no evidence to support the idea that if a bitch experiences one litter, this will soften her nature. Sixty to seventy per cent of all canine births result in the death of at least one puppy or even the bitch. If the bitch is having difficulty during labour, she may require an emergency caesarean section, and this is a significant expense for the owner and an invasive procedure for the bitch. Unwanted puppies may also need to be destroyed. These are some of the more unpleasant realities of canine pregnancy, especially if it is poorly planned.

With male dogs desexing does affect behaviour, but generally to the dog's benefit. Entire male dogs are more likely to roam searching for mates during which time they can become lost, hit by a car or fight with other dogs (see Roaming on page 174). Having your dog neutered, especially early in life, can help to curb its desire to roam and can be involved in the management of some other behaviour issues, such as dominance aggression. Castration can be surgical or chemical. Both have benefits and disadvantages, and you should discuss these with your veterinarian.

You should only keep your dog entire (undesexed) if you have real and justified intentions to breed from your dog. Many people would like to do this, but in reality very few of these people ultimately pursue this aim. As a consequence, the dog remains at risk of developing the health and behavioural problems previously mentioned. In fact, it is probably better that most of these dogs are not bred anyway, as there is already such an oversupply of dogs and plenty of suitable dogs are already being bred. It can also be very difficult to prevent unwanted matings and pregnancies, because male dogs invariably seek out female dogs on heat.

Although purebred puppies may be relatively expensive to purchase, breeding dogs is not a good way to make money. Having money-making as a primary goal can actually cause serious problems. This is because decisions involving the dogs are often motivated by money, rather than the best interests of the bitch and her puppies.

Given the health advantages and benefits of population control, if you do not plan to breed your dog, the responsible decision is to have your dog desexed or neutered, ideally as a puppy prior to sexual maturity.

4:
Building a relationship with your dog

There are well-known mental and physical health benefits for people who have a positive relationship with a pet dog. Dogs provide people with unconditional love and affection. Having a close bond with your dog helps to keep it happy too and can also help you to recognise and correct any behaviour problems that might start to develop. In order to develop such a relationship, it is important to understand that your dog is naturally a pack animal and has canine-specific mechanisms of communicating (see Chapter two).

Dogs have fairly simple needs, and most are happiest when they please their owner, the pack leader. If, for whatever reason, your dog's behaviour does not please you, the dog will not feel fulfilled. If your dog misbehaves you will tend to chastise it, even if you love your dog dearly. If this happens often, your dog may feel that it cannot do anything right. This can cause your dog to become anxious and potentially lead to a worsening of the behaviour problem (see Chapter eight). If you train your dog effectively and dedicate sufficient time and effort to correcting any unwanted problems, you will be satisfied by your dog's behaviour and will express this in praise and positive body language. This, in turn, will make your dog happier.

It is always appropriate for people to be the leaders of the household or pack and for dogs to defer and be subordinate to people (see Chapter one). If this hierarchy is not clear, problems can occur for several reasons. Firstly, the dog will be the one calling all the shots and will demand what and when things happen. It will demand attention from you, demand food from you, dictate when it is time to play, defy your commands and may climb onto furniture as it likes. It may even prevent you or other family members from sitting in certain prized places, such as the sofa or bed. It is almost impossible to teach a puppy or dog anything if it is acting as the leader of the pack.

Dominant behaviour is not just annoying or inconvenient, it can lead to the development of dominance aggression and this can be dangerous. Being the top dog is also stressful for some dogs. Thankfully, most dogs naturally defer to people. Regardless of your dog's nature, you should be the one in charge. In this role you can also be the dog's friend.

A well-loved dog is provided with good food, health care, exercise, affection and, most importantly, discipline. If you leave out the discipline, perhaps because you love your dog so much that you cannot bring yourself to chastise it, you are doing your dog a disservice. Just like children, dogs need guidelines and routine to feel secure and happy.

Sometimes people misinterpret dogs because they have human-like traits. For example, an owner who talks to their dog regularly may say that their dog knows what they are saying because of the expressions and reactions of the dog. Dogs cannot understand our spoken language.

Fortunately, most of our communication is non-verbal, just like canine communication, so dogs are very good at picking up on the sentiment of what we are saying and feeling.

Knowing your dog better can also help you to pick up any illnesses much more easily. If you know how your dog behaves when it is well, you will be able to detect any differences in its normal routine, which may indicate an illness. Aspects of behaviour that might change include: the dog's appetite, thirst, toileting habits, level of activity and its general demeanour.

Sometimes this may be as simple as a dog that is normally very naughty becoming quieter, better behaved and easier for a veterinarian to examine (see Chapter seven). Noting these changes can also help your veterinarian to investigate the dog's condition and work out how to treat the problem. *First Aid for Dogs*, Justin's first book, outlines these important aspects of your dog's routine and how to perform a basic physical examination of your dog.

People have different opinions about how a dog should be kept. Some people keep their dog outside only and do not allow it inside. Keeping a dog outside may distance it physically and emotionally from the rest of the pack, and this situation might not promote as positive a relationship between you and your dog. As people become busier and have less time for human relationships, many of us are developing a stronger relationship with our pets. Because of this, more people are choosing to keep their dog inside with the rest of the family. Also more people are keeping dogs in cities and in apartments, where there is no choice but to keep the dog inside. Further to this, there are some dog owners who allow the dog onto the couch and to sleep in the bed with them. As long as the dog's position in the pack hierarchy is clear, this is fine. However, pushy dogs will take advantage and this may cause a problem.

There are many benefits of keeping your dog inside with you. Dogs cannot tell us when they are sick. Instead we rely on the way they behave to let us know that they are unwell. Having your dog outside may mean that you do not notice a problem as easily or as early as you would if the dog was inside with you. Similarly, having your dog outside may lead to it developing behaviour issues of which you are unaware, simply because it is outside and you do not spend as much time with it. Often these sorts of problems become worse as the dog repeats the behaviour unchecked. It also means that you have less chance of correcting any behaviour problems that you do recognise. Having your dog inside promotes more contact and provides both you and your dog with more companionship and affection. Whether you share your bed with your dog or not is up to you … just make sure that the decision is up to you and not your dog!

5:
Your actions influence your dog's behaviour

How your dog behaves depends on a balance between nature and nurture. Part of your dog's behaviour is dictated by its inherent temperament, but its environment also plays a large role in how it develops. The biggest and most important environmental influence in a dog's life is you—how you act around your dog and how you treat it. You should always remember that you are top dog in the pack and so have a large amount of control and responsibility over your dog's learning.

The most powerful teaching tool you can use is positive reinforcement. Dogs learn very quickly in response to praise and encouragement and not so quickly in response to punishment. So you should use rewards to reinforce desired behaviour and a lack of praise or encouragement to discourage unwanted behaviour.

As your dog's pack leader, you also have the power to encourage undesirable behaviour inadvertently. The key is to be aware of what you are encouraging.

As the pack leader you have the power to influence your dog's behaviour in a positive way, but you can also inadvertently encourage unwanted behaviour.

When you are training your dog, it is important that you do not teach it simply a set of actions in response to your commands. It is much more useful to teach your dog to be calm while it is performing these actions. If you are teaching your dog to sit and stay, for example, you want the dog to do this in a relaxed manner rather than to have it perform the action while panting and trembling, its pupils dilated with fright. If your dog is stressed, it will not learn as effectively. For some, more relaxed dogs this comes very naturally. For many other dogs, and especially those with behaviour problems, this is not so natural. Read your dog's body language to gauge when it is anxious (see Chapter two). Be careful not to send the dog subtle signs of praise when it is stressed or aggressive, as this will encourage the wrong behaviour.

Always encourage your dog to be calm and relaxed.

Choosing a lead and collar

One of the basic tools for training your dog effectively is an appropriate lead and collar. There are various types of collars, and there is often a lot of confusion as to which is the best to have. Some people have strong views about it. Often the most important thing is that you choose what is right for you and your dog.

The standard collar and clip-on lead system gives you some control over your dog and might be fine if you have a dog that does not require physical restraint. If your dog pulls on the lead when walking or needs frequent correction for unwanted behaviour, then this system is probably not the best one for you.

Various leads and collars

A: *A choke chain*

B: *Choke chain correctly fitted*

C: *A harness and lead.*

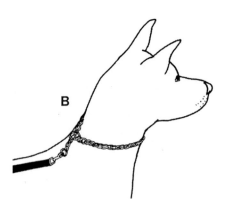

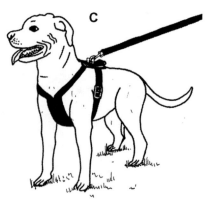

Some people prefer a harness and a clip-on lead. This has the advantage that it puts no pressure on the dog's neck and throat if it pulls when out walking. You can also thread a seatbelt through an adapter and secure the dog in the car. One disadvantage of the harness is that it gives the dog more power to pull, and some dogs will pull as if they are pulling a sled!

Choke collars can be very effective if used correctly. They should not be used as permanent collars, but as a training aid only. A short, sharp tug on the choke collar gives the dog a clear message to stop pulling on the lead because, when the dog stops pulling, the choke collar loosens. When used correctly, the

D: *A standard collar and lead*

E: *A head collar and lead*

F: *A metal pronged choke chain that digs into the dog's neck. This type of collar is cruel and not recommended.*

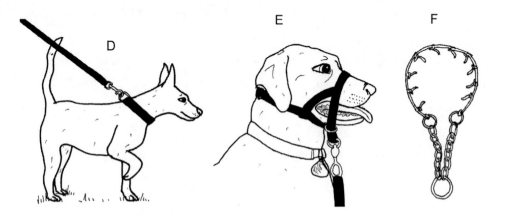

dog learns to respond to the sound of the chain moving rather than the choking action. One of the pitfalls with these collars is that some dogs constantly pull on the lead despite choking themselves. The dog does not learn to release this pressure in order to relieve itself. A similar collar is one with metal prongs, which are directed into the dog's neck. The prongs dig into the dog's skin when it pulls, causing pain. These collars may be effective in some cases, but are essentially cruel. There are many more effective training techniques which cause no pain.

The last common collar and lead system is a head collar. The collar fits over the dog's muzzle and the lead attaches under the dog's chin. Head collars are extremely useful for many dogs and in various situations. Because the lead is attached under the chin, you can lead your dog better from the front, and the head collar acts to shut the dog's mouth if it pulls too far forward on the lead. These collars give you greater control over your dog, especially a big or strong dog. Even a small tug or change in direction on the lead gives the dog a very clear message about what you would like it to do. This is important for those dogs that are not good at reading body language and other communication signals.

Lessons on learning—the canine way

Dogs learn very effectively when they are taught things using appropriate canine communication techniques. There are many books that outline various methods for training dogs. In this chapter we have summarised why a range of different techniques might be used. You have a much better chance of doing this well if you understand how your actions influence your dog's learning.

This is a complex area with terminology that can be confusing. However, the terminology is less important than understanding the underlying principles of how your actions affect your dog's behaviour.

Shaping

When you teach your dog something new, you have to start slowly and help the dog understand what you would like it to do. If your dog will not perform a set command first off, you can initially reward an action that is close to what you want it to do. For example, you can give a reward if the dog only partially squats rather than sits properly when you start teaching it to 'Sit'. Reward the dog when it improves until it is performing the task perfectly. This is known as shaping.

If your dog seems overwhelmed or is showing signs of stress when you are training it, then either take things slower and work on other things that come more easily or cut the session short. Dogs do not learn as well when they are stressed, and if you continue the session with them in this state you will inadvertently reward them for being stressed and anxious. This is counter-productive and can encourage anxiety problems.

Remember always to end the training session on a good note, even if the dog has lost interest and is not even close to performing any of the commands you are teaching. To stop a training session, ask the dog to do something simple like 'Come' or 'Sit', if it can do this reliably. Make sure the last thing you do in the session is to praise and reward your dog for good behaviour. This makes the experience enjoyable for the dog, so it is more likely to be keen for another session soon!

Conditioning and reinforcement

With conditioning, your dog associates a command with an action. Reinforcement is the stimulus that encourages your dog to make this association. This can be positive reinforcement, when you provide a reward if your dog performs correctly to your command. It can also be negative reinforcement, where you remove an unpleasant stimulus in response to good behaviour. Negative reinforcement is not punishment. Punishment involves inflicting an unpleasant action on the dog to discourage bad behaviour. An example of negative reinforcement is when a dog pulls on the lead while wearing a choke chain. As the dog pulls it feels an unpleasant choking sensation. When the dog walks properly and stops pulling, the choke chain relaxes and the unpleasant sensation stops.

Use rewards to reinforce positively desired behaviour. This motivates the dog to associate the command you gave with the action it has performed. You can reward dogs in several ways, but all work best if you give the reward a second or so after the dog has performed the desired behaviour. If you reward the dog prior to the action, it is not a reward but a bribe, and the dog is acting on its terms, not yours. Types of rewards that you can give your dog include food, pats, verbal praise, favourite chew toys and play or games. Rewarding your dog for good behaviour does not work effectively if you wait for longer than a few seconds, because the dog will not associate the reward with its actions.

Conditioning and reinforcement can be used to good effect but can also be misused. You have to be extremely careful that what you are reinforcing is good behaviour rather than inadvertently encouraging bad counterproductive behaviour. For example, if your dog is nervous and anxious when visiting the veterinarian or during a thunderstorm or fireworks display, the natural response most owners have is to comfort or even praise their dog. Unfortunately, this unintentionally acts as a reinforcer; you are saying to your dog that it is okay to be scared, it is okay to be nervous and fearful. Next time the dog is in this situation, it is likely to be more nervous, anxious and scared, because you rewarded it for this behaviour last time. This may escalate to the point that the dog develops fear aggression or hurts itself during a thunderstorm. Rather than offering comfort, using the desensitisation or counterconditioning techniques (see pages 74–75) may be more appropriate.

Rewards schedule

As discussed in Basic training techniques on page 51 most dogs are motivated to learn by food. However, some are more motivated by food than others. Make sure that treats are small enough to be concealed in your hand. You can even use a small pouch attached to your belt to carry them. A small amount of cheese or sausage is likely to be more effective than a piece of a dog's normal kibble. However, you have to be careful that the treat is not so desirable that it sends your dog into a frenzy and prevents the dog from focusing on anything else but the treat. If you feel that your dog is giving the treat more attention than you, hold it up near your face to help to establish eye contact. In extreme circumstances you can even use food rewards to provide your dog's whole nutritional requirements so the dog has to earn everything that it eats. This is how dogs that work for the police or quarantine services are managed.

If your dog is not particularly motivated by food, other types of rewards, such as attention, a favourite toy or play, may be more appropriate for your dog. Certain breeds of dog and even some individuals tend to prefer certain types of games. For example, as their names suggest, retrievers like to retrieve whereas terrier breeds tend to prefer tug-of-war type games. Make sure that you choose a game that you can win so that you maintain your position as the leader of the pack.

Regardless of the type of reward you are using, you can administer it in a rewards schedule. This can be a continuous schedule, which means that you reward the dog every time it performs the desired action correctly. This produces the fastest response, so is good to use when you are teaching your dog something new or have just started modifying its behaviour. The dog is continuously reminded of what is good behaviour. Once your dog has started to form the idea, you can switch to an intermittent rewards schedule. In this case you can either reward the dog regularly but not every time that it performs, say every third or fourth time, or you can set a more random schedule, where you reward it some of the time but not too infrequently. You can also reward the dog based on a set period of time through the training session.

Once you have taught your dog to make a link between a command, the action it performs and a reward, you can introduce what is known as a secondary reinforcer, such as praise or a clicker trainer (a training device that makes a clicking noise). This means that you not only reward your dog with a food treat, but you also praise it with a phrase such as 'Good dog!' Initially give both the primary and the secondary reinforcer together—the food reward and the praise simultaneously. Then give the food reward only some of the time but continue with the secondary reinforcer every time. Eventually your dog will associate the praise with the food, and the praise alone will bring the dog a similar level of satisfaction.

A treat pouch can be useful for holding treats when you are training your dog.

Omission training

One technique that people often overlook is rewarding their dog when it is not misbehaving. People often become focused on bad behaviour and discourage this routinely, but neglect to reward good behaviour. For example, if your dog tends to pull on the lead when walking, reward it with food and praise when it is not pulling to encourage the good behaviour. You can also introduce a command, such as 'Walk', when the dog is behaving well so the dog can associate good lead behaviour with this command and a reward. This is known as omission training.

Another example is if your dog has a barking problem. You can reward it when it is not barking and encourage the behaviour by saying the command 'Quiet' before you give the treat. It is vital that the reward comes after the good behaviour and is not a bribe to quieten the dog down, because this actually rewards the dog for barking and reinforces this unwanted behaviour.

Of course, through all this food reward positive reinforcement it is important not to let your dog become overweight!

Habituation

One very simple form of learning is called habituation. This is essentially where a dog becomes accustomed to something. For example, a puppy may become anxious and start barking the first time that it hears the telephone ring. Once the puppy experiences this more and more, and realises that this is just a normal part of life and that nothing bad will happen when the telephone rings, the anxious response will diminish. There is no need for you to become involved in this process. In fact, if you pick up the puppy to try to comfort it, you are inadvertently rewarding its anxious response.

Extinction

Another technique for stopping your dog performing an unwanted behaviour is to remove any type of reward that it might be receiving for the behaviour. This technique is known as extinction. An example of when you can use this technique is to help stop a dog from sitting around the family table at dinner time begging for table scraps. The dog most likely does this because in the past someone has given it food. If nobody gives the dog any food, no matter how long it begs or how persistent it is, the reward is removed and, hopefully, the dog will eventually give up and stop begging.

Using extinction requires you to have patience and the cooperation of everyone in the household. If someone feeds the dog at the table, even occasionally, this will act as an intermittent reward and strongly reinforce the dog's begging behaviour.

The extinction technique of training does not work well for behaviour that has an inherent reward, such as urine marking, because the dog is rewarded by the action itself, and you can't change that.

Desensitisation

The aim of this technique is to train a dog to become accustomed to something by very slowly introducing a fearful stimulus and gradually increasing its intensity, so long as the dog is not reacting inappropriately. The classic example of this is in a dog with a phobia of thunderstorms. This can be a very serious problem, as affected dogs can injure themselves in their panic (see Noise Phobia on page 103). To use desensitisation you expose the dog to a recording of a thunderstorm played at a very low volume. If the dog remains calm and does not show any signs of fear or anxiety after a period of this, praise the dog and reward it with a food treat. Gradually increase the volume for as long as the dog remains calm and relaxed, until the dog is able to be relaxed at the volume of a real thunderstorm.

Another example where desensitisation may be useful is in cases of separation anxiety (see Separation Anxiety on page 93). Many dogs with separation anxiety become distressed when the owner prepares to leave the house. If your dog does this, leave the house for a brief time only, then come back inside. This way the dog starts to learn that you will not always be gone for a long time and that you will come back. You can gradually increase the period of time that you are out of the house, as long as your dog does not become overly stressed or anxious. Eventually your dog will be less anxious when you leave.

Counterconditioning

In this technique when the dog starts to perform an undesirable behaviour, you command it to perform another positive behaviour that it has already learnt and knows that you will reward it for. This is usually something very simple like 'Sit'. If your dog has an aggression problem, for example, command it to 'Sit' as soon as it starts to show signs of aggression, then reward it with food and praise once it can sit in a calm and relaxed manner. The desire to please you and perform this positive behaviour will eventually compete with and substitute the problem aggressive behaviour.

This technique can be coupled with desensitisation. For example, when trying to desensitise a dog to thunderstorms, you can command the dog to 'Sit' then reward the dog it if does not show signs of fear or anxiety as the volume increases. Counterconditioning distracts the dog from the anxiety by persuading it to focus on a pleasant behaviour it knows it will be rewarded for.

As you repeat this training, the dog's fear should reduce until it has no anxiety response to the particular stimulus. For this method to be effective, you have to be very patient and progress very slowly. If you increase the intensity of the stimulation too quickly, the dog will start to become overly stressed and you will end up inadvertently rewarding its fear and anxiety.

Flooding

Another approach some people advocate to change a dog's fearful response to a particular stimulus is called flooding. This technique is very different to desensitisation or counterconditioning. Flooding is considered as a last resort if other safer techniques do not work. With flooding you confine the dog to a small area, such as a small room or a large crate, and expose it to the offending stimulus, such as the sound of a thunderstorm, at a high intensity for a prolonged period of time. You continue this despite the dog's distress, until the dog gives up its anxious response. This may take a long time. While this is going on, nobody should have any contact or interaction with the dog.

There are some quite serious risks associated with flooding such as making the original anxiety problem worse, so you should not use it unless it is under the direct advice and supervision of an animal behaviourist, veterinarian or veterinary behaviourist and even then only as a last resort.

Punishment

Along with the other methods of training described above, you can use punishment cautiously to help to correct unwanted behaviour problems. Punishment does not have to be physical or necessarily painful. Punishment can be as simple as banishing a dog to a 'sin bin' for a period of time. A 'sin bin' is a place where the dog is isolated and receives no attention, such as a laundry or garage. The 'sin bin' should not be a place where the dog is fed or where training occurs. Punishment can be verbal in the form of stern words such as 'No!' or 'Bad dog!' This should be delivered in an assertive manner. Alternatively it can be an unpleasant sensation such as spraying the dog with a water jet.

Regardless of the method, for punishment to be effective, just like rewards and reinforcement it must be executed immediately, preferably within a few seconds and definitely not beyond 30 to 60 seconds after the unwanted behaviour. If the punishment is not delivered immediately, the dog will not associate the punishment with the bad behaviour. This will lead to the dog feeling that it is being punished randomly, which can cause it to become stressed and inhibit its learning.

Punishment should be brief. If your dog misbehaved in the morning, there is no point holding a grudge, being angry with it and continuing the punishment when you come home in the afternoon. The dog will not know what you are upset about and will not make the connection with the atrocity it committed eight hours prior. Dogs do not hold grudges against other pack members and nor should you. Similarly your dog will not resent you for punishing it or for withholding food or treats until it behaves well such as sitting calmly. The aim of punishment is to startle the dog so it stops the undesirable behaviour and, hopefully, to reduce the chance of it repeating the behaviour in the future.

Punishment must be consistent. A dog should be punished every time it performs the unwanted behaviour. This means everyone in the house should be committed to and involved in the dog's behaviour modification. Ideally, punishment should be followed by a command for positive behaviour, such as sitting calmly, so you can reward the dog and remind it what good behaviour is.

If you are using punishment, you should also try to remember to reward your dog when it is not misbehaving. It is no fun for you or your dog if you are constantly punishing it. You will find that the more you are able to reward and reinforce good behaviour, the less that you will have to use punishment to deter bad behaviour.

Punishment needs to be used very carefully, because if it is not used in appropriate situations, with the correct timing, or if it is not executed properly, it can be counterproductive. Punishment of overly nervous or fearful dogs is inappropriate, because this will only add to their anxiety. It may even cause them to develop fear aggression. Extreme caution needs to be taken when punishing a dog with dominance aggression because your punishment may be seen as a challenge and the dog may respond with aggression towards you (see Chapter ten). Also physical punishment has the potential to seriously and even permanently injure your dog, especially when it is a puppy.

Electric shock collars are a form of physical punishment and can be operated remotely or triggered by barking. When they are used for barking problems, they deliver the punishment swiftly and consistently, and the punishment does not persist significantly beyond the dog stopping the unwanted behaviour. However, they have the potential to make some problems worse and should only be used under the direct advice of an animal behaviourist, veterinarian or veterinary behaviourist. They are also not legal in all areas. Citronella spray collars may be more appropriate, because they provide an unpleasant punishment but not a painful or overly frightening one. Again these should be used under professional advice (see Chapter eleven).

Avoidance

For some behaviour problems the most practical and safest solution is simply to avoid the stimulus that triggers the behaviour. For example, if your dog eats its own stools or other animal's stools, such as horse manure, the reward that the dog finds in this behaviour may be very strong and it can be very difficult to deter. It may be easier for you to make sure that you pick up your dog's stools as soon as possible or avoid contact with other stools it might eat. Often puppies grow out of this behaviour (see Eating abnormal objects on page 112).

Another example of where avoidance may help is if your dog has a fear of something that happens infrequently, such as the sound of a balloon popping. You could embark on a desensitisation and counterconditioning program, or you could simply avoid popping or even holding balloons around your dog. Avoiding triggers for undesirable behaviour is especially important when you are teaching your dog an alternative, positive behaviour, such as to sit in a relaxed manner. The dog should be focused on you and not have any distractions. Exposure to any trigger of misbehaviour when your dog is focusing on you could be counterproductive.

Professional advice

For more severe behaviour problems that you cannot solve yourself, you should consult an animal behaviourist, veterinarian or veterinary behaviourist. In some instances medication may need to be considered to help with the problem, at least initially. Drugs may be helpful for problems that have an underlying anxiety disorder, including aggression (see Chapters eight, nine and ten). Medications can also be useful for dogs with abnormal repetitive behaviour, similar to obsessive compulsive disorders in people (see Chapter nine).

Typically medication is introduced at a loading dose, then is slowly tapered to a maintenance dose, or even discontinued if there is a significant improvement in the problem behaviour. Drugs usually need to be used in conjunction with a behaviour modification program and always under the close instruction of a veterinarian or veterinary behaviourist.

6:
Other animals influence your dog's behaviour

The other animals in your home, your neighbourhood, in the park and at the veterinary clinic can influence your dog's behaviour in various ways. They may, for example, elicit a submissive or even fearful response. Your dog may become protective of its territory, its food or its pack members, including you, around other animals. Your dog may have a confrontation with another animal if they are of a similar rank. Other animals may distract your dog and this can elicit bad behaviour or affect training sessions with you. This can happen even if they are not directly interacting with your dog. It may even be enough for a dog to walk past a window of your house for your dog to divert its focus away from you and the training.

However, the presence of other dogs can sometimes be beneficial in training your dog. Dogs might form alliances with you and feel more confident and dominant when they are with you, often more so when they are on a lead. Similarly dogs can form alliances with other dogs. Fearful or anxious dogs may benefit from having more confident dogs around because they can follow their lead and be more relaxed. Very stoic dogs, such as a placid old Labrador Retriever, can be used to help desensitise a dog with interdog aggression. Because the stoic older dog is unlikely to respond or react in any way, the reactive dog learns that it gains nothing by being aggressive (see Chapter ten).

If your dog is more submissive, or overly fearful, an approach from another dog could trigger active defence and retaliation or fear aggression. As we discussed in Chapter one, the pack is a very dynamic unit and, while a dog may be submissive in one scenario, it might be much more confident in another.

If your dog associates frequently with another dog of a similar confidence level or degree of dominance, this situation could result in a conflict. If neither wants to back down from its position, the encounter then escalates. In these cases using a rank reduction program to reduce the hierarchy of the lower-ranking dog in the pack can help to reduce conflicts (see Chapter one). Sometimes the cause of the conflict may be a combination of the similar rank position and also their individual willingness to protect a prized possession such as food, a special toy, their owner or their favourite place to sleep. Even a dog that is usually not so confident may be prepared to challenge another dog of a higher rank over something that is important to it.

Sometimes other animals may trigger bad behaviour. The classic example of this is interdog aggression, in which the offending dog may become anxious at the sight, sound or smell of another dog and will tend to react in an unreasonable and aggressive way. Dogs that have interdog aggression commonly have an underlying anxiety problem, which may only manifest in the presence of another dog. Another typical example is that of a cat running away, and this can often be an irresistible temptation for a dog to give chase. This can be a serious issue as the cat is at risk of being mauled by the dog. The dog is also at risk of injury because a cat can scratch a dog's eye badly. Also if the dog is focused on chasing the cat, it may accidentally run into the path of an oncoming car.

Dogs hunt in packs so sometimes they are more likely to pursue another cat or attack another dog at the park when they are in a group. It is important to be aware of this pack-hunting phenomenon because these group attacks can be especially brutal.

Given the influence that other animals can have on your dog and the dynamic nature of the pack structure, introducing new pets to the household can cause problems. The new pet may temporarily upset the pack hierarchy and conflict may result until a new pack hierarchy is established. However, new pets can have positive effects on your dog's behaviour, providing companionship and reducing boredom. Sometimes if animals from a household are separated, for example if one is hospitalised, reintroducing it back into the household can also be stressful.

The key to introducing a new pet or reintroducing a pet is to take things slowly and to have patience. Firstly ensure that both your dog and the new pet are healthy, fully vaccinated and up to date with flea control and worm prevention. Your house and yard should be secure, so that neither your dog nor the new pet can run away. A new pet is likely to be very inquisitive of its new environment, especially if it is young, so you should ensure that the environment is safe and that the new pet does not have access to hazards such as toxins. Refer to Justin's previous books, *First Aid for Dogs* and *First Aid for Cats,* for more information on keeping your pets safe.

You should not change your dog's routine too much when you introduce a new pet. Initially the new pet may need to have restricted access to certain areas of the house. You should introduce a new pet dog to your dog on neutral ground, not in your dog's favourite areas, such as near its bed, as your dog may see this as a threat to its territory. Both dogs should be on a lead initially so you can control them and assess each dog's response. It is natural for your dog and other existing pets to investigate the new arrival and you should allow this, initially in a closely supervised fashion. Allowing your dog to interact with the new animal unsupervised too early can be dangerous. Give each of the dogs your undivided attention for short periods of time, without any other animals around. This will help to strengthen your relationship with the two dogs and maintain your position as the leader of the pack.

Another potential area of conflict is the feeding area. Initially feed the pets separately. You can very gradually move the bowls closer together. If there are any signs of hostility, move the bowls back to where they were located when there was not a problem and maintain this location for a week or so, then start trying to slowly move the bowls closer together.

Whenever your dog interacts with the new dog, read their body language (see page 23) and try to detect any signs of hostility. At the first sign of aggression startle the dogs with a loud sound or a squirt with a water pistol. This should ideally occur within a few seconds, but certainly within 30 to 60 seconds of the dogs showing signs of hostility. If there is a clear aggressor, banish that dog to an area such as a laundry or bathroom designated the 'sin bin'. Then ask the victim to sit in a calm and relaxed way. Only then should you reassure the dog by patting it soothingly. Be careful that you do not reassure the dog too early and inadvertently encourage anxious fearful behaviour (see Chapter five).

Despite all your efforts, not all dogs and other pets will be compatible or live happily together. Sometimes animals just tend to ignore each other and have minimal interaction. This is fine as long as it does not cause anxiety.

Sometimes animals just will not tolerate each other and end up fighting often, which can be a serious problem. Conflict can sometimes be improved by addressing the particular aggression problem (see Chapter ten) or introducing a rank reduction program (see Chapter one). If even your most diligent efforts are not successful, consult an animal behaviourist, veterinarian, or veterinary behaviourist, who may recommend medication to help. Unfortunately, in some cases the best solution for you, your dog and the new animal may be to re-home one or more of the pets.

7:
Illness can influence your dog's behaviour

If your dog is unwell, it can affect the way that it behaves. This can lead to unwanted behaviour such as urinating in the house or your dog becoming aggressive. Having a good awareness of your dog's normal behaviour and its normal appetite, activity levels and toileting habits can help you to identify any medical problems so you can seek veterinary care for your dog.

If your dog is in pain it may be very obvious, and the dog may cry out or try to bite you if you touch it. This is especially true of acutely painful conditions such as a neck or back injury, although the source of the pain may be hard to determine. This response is not necessarily indicative of aggression. The biting response is appropriate because the dog is trying to protect itself from further pain. Pain can also come on slowly, can be subtle and can cause vague behaviour changes. An example of this is arthritis, which usually occurs in older dogs, causing them to slow down, lose their spark and even become crankier. If a dog has been in pain for a long time, it may have learned to be scared of people touching it where it hurts. For example, a dog with a sore eye may become 'head shy', and this may persist even after the painful eye condition is treated and has resolved.

One of the most common ailments dogs can suffer is itchy skin disease. This can have many causes, including fleas, mites, infection with bacteria or yeast and, possibly most commonly, by an allergy. These skin diseases can cause dogs to chew themselves over various sites, lick themselves, scratch, rub their belly or face on the ground or their back on objects. If the licking continues for an extended period of time, it can lead to what is known as an acral lick granuloma. Sometimes excessive licking can be a manifestation of an abnormal behaviour problem so behaviour modification can be part of the treatment in conjunction with medical therapy (see Licking, chewing and self-mutilation on page 115).

If the skin problem involves the ears, a dog may shake its head excessively as well as rub and scratch the area. If the problem involves blocked or infected anal sacs the dog may scoot its bottom along the ground. Sometimes itchy skin conditions can make a dog very anxious and restless, or it may do things suddenly like leap out of bed in a panicked state if a flea bites it.

Often itchy skin conditions are associated with changes to the skin such as bald areas, redness, sores and rashes or pimple-type lesions, but this is not always the case and some dogs can be very itchy with fairly normal-looking skin. Itchy skin can be very frustrating for both you and your dog, and if your dog is suffering from this you should take it to see your veterinarian.

Many conditions can increase your dog's thirst, including diabetes and other hormonal conditions and kidney and liver problems. Specific medications such as steroids, anti-convulsants for epilepsy and diuretics used in heart conditions can also increase your dog's thirst. Occasionally a behaviour problem can be the cause of increased thirst. Increased water consumption is usually associated with increased urine production. This can lead to your dog urinating in the house, despite being well toilet trained. Dogs with reduced mobility, such as those with arthritis, may be more likely to urinate in the house if they have increased urine production and cannot access outside easily. It is easy to mistake these accidents for laziness or misbehaviour. Other urinary conditions such as infections, bladder stones or tumours and incontinence can also lead to accidents in the house. A medical condition needs to be ruled out before you start punishing your dog for these accidents and pursuing behaviour modification.

Medical conditions, such as hormonal or gastrointestinal conditions, and even some medications, such as steroids and anti-convulsants for epilepsy, can increase your dog's appetite. This can cause your dog to constantly beg for food, steal food and scavenge for food off the street or from rubbish bins. This can be very frustrating and can also be detrimental to your dog's health because the dog may become overweight, ingest spoilt food, toxins or foreign objects, such as toys or clothes, which can cause life-threatening bowel obstructions. It is easy to become angry with a dog that is constantly begging you for food if you think that it is just being naughty. However, it may be that it has a medical reason for the increase in appetite so you should take your dog to see your veterinarian.

Pregnancy can cause an increase in your dog's appetite for obvious reasons, but it can also cause other behaviour changes. Some dogs can experience a false or pseudo-pregnancy after heat, which mimics true pregnancy but with no puppies. Towards the end of pregnancy or of false pregnancy, you may notice some changes to the bitch's behaviour. Some bitches do not show any maternal behaviour but others are quite obvious. You might notice nest-making activities, including digging, tearing of clothing and bedding and burying certain objects. Some bitches also can develop maternal aggression (see Maternal aggression on page 154). In healthy bitches, these behaviour changes usually subside with time and especially with weaning of the puppies.

Sometimes behaviour changes are due to neurological or brain disease. These changes can be things such as staring into space, disorientation and inability to recognise you, general dullness, or that your dog simply is just not right. These changes can be accompanied by other physical signs such as a droopy face, the inability to blink one or both eyes, blindness, loss of balance, a tilted head, stumbling or an uncoordinated or drunken-type gait, circling compulsively in one direction and pressing the head into a corner. Severe liver failure can cause similar behaviour changes. If you feel that your dog has had any change in its behaviour you should take it to see your veterinarian.

A common question that people ask is 'why do dogs eat grass?' There is no simple answer to this, but illness such as an upset stomach can play a role.

Dogs are omnivorous animals so it is normal for them to eat some vegetation. Some plants can help to control intestinal parasites, so this is another potential reason. It may also be that the dog is trying to include more roughage or fibre in its diet.

Wild dogs ingest a lot of bone and hair in their natural diet, which they may not be able to digest. Vomiting can help to bring these items up. Dogs are very good at vomiting and can vomit almost voluntarily. Eating grass can assist this. Dogs that have bones stuck in their food pipe or oesophagus become very distressed and regularly retch and try to vomit. When we have had to remove a bone that has become stuck in a dog's food pipe or oesophagus, there have almost always been several blades of grass sitting in front of the bone.

Part of the reason dogs eat grass may also be as simple as that a dog may have seen another dog eating grass so it mimics this behaviour. Dogs are inquisitive animals and curiosity may also be part of the reason. Eating other unusual items is discussed further in Eating abnormal objects on page 112.

8:
Canine anxiety

Dogs are not people, but they can suffer from many similar health issues, including anxiety problems. You may have heard of people having anxiety or panic attacks, but you may not appreciate that a very similar condition can also affect our canine companions. In fact, more dogs have anxiety problems than many people recognise, and the majority of behaviour issues we have outlined in this book can be initiated or exacerbated by anxiety. Anxiety disorders are caused by a neurochemical imbalance in the brain.

Canine anxiety is common and underpins many canine behaviour problems.

Why is canine anxiety so common? One of the likely reasons is that domestic dogs have retained many of the natural instincts of their wild ancestors, but they are now in a completely different environment. It is easy to forget to allow dogs to be dogs. Through love and sometimes ignorance, some people treat dogs like they are small people, and this can be very confusing for a dog. That does not mean that dogs today would prefer to live in the wild or that they do not appreciate the love that their owners give them. Dogs are very well suited to domestication and we have made them man's best friend, with mutual benefits for dogs and people.

Another issue that may contribute to the high incidence of canine anxiety is that in the past, people have bred dogs largely for their appearance rather than selecting specifically for temperament. Generally breeders have not been selecting for calm, relaxed or less anxious dogs. Dogs have been bred to look good, conform to the breed standards and perform well in the show ring. Because they look good, such dogs are often selected for breeding only and may pass on any nervous characteristics to their offspring. To be fair, this is certainly not the case for all breeds, and some breeders now are actively trying to breed more for desirable temperament, leading to more suitable pets.

Anxious dogs appear apprehensive and are always anticipating danger. They might have increased awareness, be very active and seem to spend a lot of time scanning their environment for danger. The signs are not always obvious and can progress in a very subtle way. Sometimes the first thing people notice is urine in the house or trembling when other people visit the house. It is important to realise that anxious dogs do not always tremble or have their tail between their legs, with their head and ears down. They can be relaxed and calm and behave like completely normal dogs in situations that they trust. This is where they are not fearful of the people, and there are no strange noises or activities to make them stressed, but certain situations may trigger their anxiety.

The situations which trigger anxiety can be hard for people to spot, so it may seem like the dog is behaving very well one minute but then may misbehave for no apparent reason, by urinating in the house for example. When a dog is anxious it usually looks sheepish and may cower, and this can lead to an owner thinking that 'it knows he has done the wrong thing'. It may just be that the timid behaviour is due to his anxiety rather than misbehaviour. The fearful behaviour may be exacerbated if you become angry with the dog for its behaviour.

Anxiety problems are very complicated, and every dog with anxiety behaves differently. Unfortunately, no matter how well you train your dog as a puppy, some dogs always go on to develop anxiety and related behaviour problems. Just like people, childhood experiences and certain backgrounds can cause obsessive and compulsive disorder (OCD) or other behaviour disorders as adults. How the dog turns out is not all your fault. However, prevention is always better than cure. If you start out on the right foot when your dog is a puppy, you have the best chance of preventing anxiety and other behaviour problems later in life (see Chapter three).

Separation anxiety

In this well-known type of anxious behaviour, dogs become extremely distressed when they are left alone. This might be when they are left alone in the house or in the yard when the family goes out. In some extreme cases, it can also occur if a dog is locked in a room alone, even if there are people in the very next room. The signs of separation anxiety vary from dog to dog and can be subtle. Some signs are obvious like barking and destructive behaviour, but others are more subtle like whimpering, pacing or drooling. A tape recorder, video camera or webcam set up when you go out can help to give you an idea of what your dog actually does when you leave the house, and this can help you decide if your dog has separation anxiety.

A typical scenario of separation anxiety starts when the family is preparing to leave the house. Your dog can pick up on cues, such as the fact that school and work bags may be out, you may wear particular clothes, you may handle keys and you may shut windows and close various doors. The dog associates these cues with stress, because it has learnt that these signals occur when it is left alone. The dog may start to become anxious, pace or show alert behaviour like having its ears pricked or it might vocalise and whine. You might notice that the dog starts to follow you everywhere you go. Many people interpret this as being cute and affectionate, but actually it is a sign that the dog is already anxious and cannot relax. In most cases the family will notice that the dog is distressed and try to comfort it, pat it and talk softly to it before leaving the house. Although these actions come naturally, these attempts to comfort the dog do not calm it down. Instead, comforting your dog at this time actually gives it a strong message that you approve of its distress and anxiety. This inadvertently encourages its anxiety and anxious behaviour.

Although it may come naturally, do not praise or try to calm your dog when it is being anxious. This will only reinforce the anxious behaviour.

Once the family has left the house the dog's anxiety increases further. The most common behaviour that dogs with separation anxiety show is increased vocalisation. This might be howling, barking or whining. Anxious dogs might also go to the toilet in the house, often in many different locations. This is not to punish their owners but is a result of their distress. Some dogs become so frantic when they are left alone they can destroy the entire garden or house and may even be able to scratch right through the door that confines them. Again the dog does not cause destruction to punish its owner, it is the dog's way of trying to cope. Another dog might try to escape, in an attempt to find the family, other dogs or people so that it is no longer alone. Some dogs will direct the destructive behaviour at themselves. They might repeat an action over and over again as a way to cope with being alone such as licking or chewing themselves excessively (see Chapter nine).

Obviously destructive behaviour is frustrating and unacceptable, so most dogs are disciplined when the family arrives home, by being yelled at, sent outside or physically punished. Unfortunately, too much time has passed by this stage, so your dog cannot associate the punishment with its actions hours before. Actually the punishment only serves to make the dog's anxiety worse, and it may become fearful of you. Sometimes people notice their dog cowering as soon as they come home and assume that this is an admission by the dog that it 'knew it had done something wrong'. However, the dog is behaving like this because it is anxious and because it is responding to your angry body language. The dog cannot associate its previous actions with your anger.

In milder cases of separation anxiety, the dog may have spent the entire time trembling and drooling. When the family arrives home, they find the dog super-excited to see them and inadvertently excite the dog further by talking to it or patting it enthusiastically or even giving it a food treat. These actions just reinforce to the dog that it is great to have you at home and that all this enthusiasm and attention will disappear if you leave it home alone.

It is important to understand that normal, relaxed, easygoing dogs cope very well when they are left alone. Most dogs sleep or watch the outside world through a window or fence. If you start out on the right foot by teaching your puppy that it is not a major problem when you leave the house, then you have the best chance of preventing it developing separation anxiety.

Reducing your dog's separation anxiety

You should always have your dog evaluated by your veterinarian to identify possible medical problems that may cause signs of anxiety.

Do not pat or comfort your dog when it appears distressed. It feels natural to comfort your dog, but doing this inadvertently sends a strong message to your dog that you approve of its behaviour. You actually encourage its stress by praising the worried, stressful behaviour. Instead, completely ignore the dog until it is sitting calmly and quietly. Only give your dog attention when it is behaving in a calm and relaxed way.

Do not pay the dog any attention when you arrive home. This can be difficult because often the dog will be overexcited and jump or bark with excitement, and you will also naturally be pleased to see your canine companion. However, if you respond to your dog's excited behaviour by talking to it and patting it, you are inadvertently reinforcing that it needs you to be around all the time. Instead, you should completely ignore your dog when you come home. This means not talking to it, touching it or even looking at it. After a period of time, the dog will settle down and sit quietly and calmly. At this stage, you should pay it attention by praising the good, relaxed behaviour.

Do not punish your dog when you arrive home, no matter how bad the damage to the house is. Dogs associate punishment with their own behaviour for only a few seconds after they have performed the inappropriate behaviour. You have no chance of teaching a dog that it was wrong to destroy the house when you discover the damage hours after the event. Unless you catch your dog in the act of being destructive, urinating in the house or barking, punishment will not help to teach it that the behaviour was inappropriate.

Try to reduce the stress associated with you leaving the house. Every family has a routine when they leave the house and within this routine, there are several cues that the dog will associate with stress and the family leaving, such as the sound of the keys or the windows shutting. To reduce your dog's stress, you can reduce the number of cues. For example, you could pack the schoolbags outside, or separate the house keys so they do not make noise when they are handled. Shut the windows and doors some time before you leave. You can also try leaving through a different door. Further to this, you can give your dog a treat when you shut the windows and doors, so it starts to associate it with an enjoyable experience, but be careful not to give the treat if your dog is distressed. Ask the dog to sit and be relaxed, then give it a treat. Also, you can perform these routines at times on the weekend when you are not leaving the house. Put on your work clothes on the weekend when you are at home or even take your dog for a walk in them so it associates them with good things rather than you leaving.

When you do leave your dog at home, ensure it has something to keep it occupied, such as toys. We do not recommend you leave your dog alone with a bone for safety reasons. Too many times we have had to treat dogs with bones caught in their mouth, throat or intestines. You should always be there to prevent your dog eating or chewing on small sharp fragments of bone. An indestructible toy in which you can hide food keeps most dogs occupied for hours. Also, many dogs are more relaxed when they are left alone with some low-level noise such as the television or radio.

You can also try locking your dog in a room where it feels more comfortable when you go out. This needs to be a place where the dog feels calm and relaxed. You can actively encourage this by rewarding the dog whenever it is calm and relaxed in a particular room. This room should be a place where your dog has had positive experiences, such as training and rewards or being fed. If you have crate-trained your dog, you can use their crate as the place where your dog feels comfortable. Regardless, the area should never be used as a 'sin bin' where the dog is banished when it misbehaves. The room should be well lit, have a comfortable bed and access to food and water. Some dogs do much better if they are left in a room where they can observe the outside world. Other dogs cope better if they can be left outside. If your dog has been crate-trained, you could place it outside so the dog is still safe and sheltered from the sun, wind and rain. As well as making the room a place where your dog feels comfortable you should also 'puppy-proof' the room by removing *anything* the dog can destroy, including power cords, furniture, mats etc.

When you are leaving your dog, gradually expose it to longer and longer periods of time alone. Start slowly with a short period, say five minutes in a room by itself, when you are in the next room. Do this four to five times a day on the weekend when you are at home. Gradually increase the time to ten minutes, fifteen minutes and then thirty minutes. When you let your dog out, do not pay it any attention. Making a fuss of your dog by greeting it with excitement reinforces to your dog that it is much better to have you around and increases the separation anxiety. Once your dog has settled down or can sit or lie calmly, praise it and give it a treat. Ignoring the initial excitement gives the message that coming and going is part of the normal routine, and over time your dog will be less concerned about being left alone.

You should consult with your veterinarian about your dog's separation anxiety. He or she might recommend a suitable anti-anxiety medication. Medication can be used to facilitate your dog's learning by reducing anxiety. Using medication at the same time as behaviour modification techniques can help your dog to learn more rapidly. Over a period of a few months, you may be able to gradually reduce and even discontinue the medication under the guidance of your veterinarian.

Attention-seeking behaviour

Anxious dogs commonly require more attention than other dogs. Most of the time dogs with anxiety are not good at understanding normal day-to-day signals from their environment. They cannot distinguish well between a threatening situation and non-threatening situation. For example a normal, less anxious dog is good at reading the body language of other dogs and strange people quickly, so it can determine if the dog or person is friendly or not. An anxious dog may not be as good at reading these signals and may feel fear and anxiety because it does not know how it should react to the new dog or person.

Sometimes the cause for anxiety is not obvious or even rational. Some dogs have anxiety that is triggered by change of any type. One such dog we treated became extremely anxious about some new turf that was laid in its yard. Another dog became extremely anxious when the kettle was put on. These dogs cannot rationalise that there is no threat to them. They are not good at reading the signals from their environment and determining what is safe and what is not. For this reason dogs with anxiety may constantly need to seek reassurance from their owner that everything is safe.

Attention-seeking behaviour can appear very different for individual dogs. The more common ways to gain attention include nudging, pawing or barking. Some dogs sit and stare, whine, cry or howl at their owner and very often this type of behaviour earns the dog its owner's attention. Even if the attention is negative, like yelling at the dog, the dog has received attention and the dog's craving for attention is satisfied for a short time. Shortly after this the attention-seeking may start again because the dog again needs regular reassurance that the environment is safe and there is no threat. Sometimes these more typical ways to gain attention do not work or the dog needs more attention than the owner can possibly provide. In these circumstances, the dog may start to use abnormal behaviour, such as tail chasing, as a way to attract attention (see Chapter nine: Abnormal repetitive behaviour on page 108).

Remember that some degree of attention-seeking is a normal part of the interaction between dogs and also between dogs and people. It is a natural way for dogs to communicate. All dogs will seek attention and interact with people by pawing, nudging or barking to some degree. After they receive attention, play a game or receive a scratch, most normal dogs will be satisfied and stop the behaviour. More anxious dogs will not be satisfied and will continue to bark or nudge their owner. This constant attention-seeking quickly becomes a burden for the people to whom it is directed and this needs to be addressed.

Reducing attention-seeking behaviour

Never let your dog dictate when it receives attention. By responding to your dog every time it barks, paws at you or nudges you, you are reinforcing the attention-seeking behaviour. It may seem affectionate and cute, but nudging can be distracting and annoying if it becomes constant, especially while you are trying to concentrate on something else. It can also prevent you carrying out daily activities if there is a dog always under your feet. Encouraging mild attention-seeking behaviour can also cause it to become more severe.

Be observant so that you can identify when your dog is seeking attention. Dogs can be very subtle, especially when the typical behaviours like barking, pawing or nudging have failed. You may find that your dog simply leans on you and gains attention by the subconscious fall of your hand to pat it or even by the general movement of your legs. So you need to be very aware of how your actions can so easily give your dog the attention it is seeking and further encourage this behaviour.

You can try to reduce your dog's attention-seeking behaviour by completely ignoring it. This works, in many but not all cases, by removing any chance of positively reinforcing the behaviour. Over time the dog will learn that it cannot dictate when it receives attention and stop asking for it. As well as ignoring your dog's attention-seeking behaviour, it is important to praise and reward it when it is behaving well.

Be aware that it is easy to give your dog attention inadvertently, and, for some dogs, even punishment can satisfy the need for attention.

However, some dogs with attention-seeking problems may grow worse if they are completely ignored, because their underlying anxiety is not alleviated. Some dogs will resort to abnormal and possibly destructive behaviour to attract attention if their more typical methods fail. This is stressful for both you and the dog, and it is not good for your relationship.

Another method is to teach your dog another, more acceptable behaviour in order to attract attention such as sitting calmly. Firstly you must walk away from your dog when it is seeking attention. Ignore it by becoming very still. If it leaves you alone, continue your previous activity. If it stops and looks at you or sits down, you must praise it. You are praising the calm and relaxed behaviour and giving the dog attention on your terms. You can also ask your dog to sit when it is seeking attention. If it does, you can praise it after a few seconds of sitting in a calm, relaxed way. If it does not sit or is behaving in a very anxious way, you must walk away and become still again, ignoring the dog. Eventually the dog will follow you in order to gain attention. You can repeat the request for it to sit. Eventually the dog will do as it is asked in order to get attention and will learn over time that the only way it receives attention is when it is sitting quietly and calmly.

Modifying the behaviour of dogs with attention-seeking behaviour takes a lot of patience, perseverance and consistency. You will need to practise with your dog regularly and there are no quick-fixes—success will not happen overnight. Initially you will need to practise the above techniques many times a day. Over time, you can reduce the frequency of your praise, so that your dog does not receive attention every time it is sitting calmly. Intermittent rewards and attention are often enough to maintain the dog's understanding.

You should also consult with your veterinarian for guidance on reducing your dog's attention-seeking behaviour. Sometimes anti-anxiety medication can help if used in conjunction with the behaviour-modifying techniques described above. Once you can make it through the day without your dog seeking attention on its terms, you may be able to gradually reduce and even discontinue the medication under the guidance of your veterinarian. You do, however, need to be vigilant with the behaviour-modification techniques in the long term, and some anxious dogs may benefit with medication.

Noise phobia

Some dogs show extreme fear when they hear certain sounds. The most common sounds that dogs fear are thunderstorms and fireworks, and it is always sad to see just how many dogs escape from their yard by frantic climbing or digging in fear when they hear such sounds. Some of these dogs are unlucky and end up at the veterinary hospital after they have been involved a road-traffic accident or suffered some other misadventure. Noise phobia is similar to panic disorders in people. Dogs with noise phobia become extremely anxious and frantic when they hear the trigger noise.

Reducing your dog's fear during a storm

You should not try to comfort your dog during a thunderstorm. This is often difficult, because you may see your dog shivering in a corner and our natural instincts tell us to help the dog. However, by comforting the dog during these times, you are actually inadvertently encouraging its distressed, fearful behaviour; you are telling it that it is okay to be scared. There are more appropriate alternative methods for making your dog more comfortable, which are suggested below.

You should also definitely not punish your dog when it is fearful. You may wish to discourage its frantic behaviour, but punishing the dog will only cause it to become more anxious and therefore more distressed. It may also learn to associate the trigger noise with being punished as well as feeling fear. Next time the noise occurs, the behaviour may be worse.

It is better to ignore the dog while it is showing the fearful behaviour, unless it is causing itself harm. Always make sure that your dog is in a safe environment during a storm, perhaps in a room where it cannot damage itself or the room. In the long term you can help your dog to become accustomed to thunderstorms using desensitisation or distract it from its fear and encourage an alternative, more appropriate behaviour with counterconditioning (see Chapter five).

Consult with your veterinarian throughout the behaviour-modification process. Initially dogs may be unmanageable when they hear the trigger noise. Your veterinarian may prescribe medication to help your dog to relax during these fearful times. In most cases the best time to give the medication is before the fearful noise starts. This is sometimes impossible, for example, when a storm comes quickly or you are at work. Also, dogs can often hear the storm before we can. However, sometimes you can be prepared, such as when fireworks are planned for a festive event. In more severe cases of noise phobia, the dog may benefit from anti-anxiety medication while you are practising desensitisation. The medication dose may be able to be reduced or even discontinued as the dog progresses.

You should not attempt to use flooding (see page 76), which involves continuously exposing your dog to the noise it fears, as a behaviour-modification technique. It is very controversial and not one we recommend, unless it is performed under the direct advice and supervision of a behaviourist, veterinarian or veterinary behaviourist, usually as a last resort. If done incorrectly or with the wrong dog it can be inhumane and can make the dog's anxiety and fear much worse.

Fear

Dogs can be fearful of anything at all. Irrational fear is usually a sign that the dog has an underlying anxiety problem. Fears can be directed at people, other animals or objects. For example, the family dog may fear only one of the family members, even if there is absolutely no history of punishment, violence or abuse. This can be particularly distressing, because that family member may feel isolated and guilty that the dog is fearful of them. It is not the person's fault and it is the dog's anxiety which needs addressing.

A dog may have had a fearful experience in the past, which it associates with any event that is similar. For example, if balloon pops close to a puppy's face, it may develop a phobia of balloons in any context. If a dog was abused as a puppy or at a previous home, it may fear anyone who looks similar to the abuser. It may even be fearful of all people. It is useful to know if the fear relates to a particular event in the past so you can try to desensitise your dog to that fear. This is not always possible because an accurate history is not available for many rescue dogs.

Reducing fear

Managing generalised fear is very similar to management of noise phobia. Firstly, it is important to identify the trigger. Is it the fact that the person is male, or is it because he is carrying a briefcase? Is it other dogs or just male dogs? Knowing your dog well and recognising when its body language changes from relaxation to fear will help you to determine the trigger.

A practical approach is sometimes as simple as avoiding the trigger. For example, if your dog is fearful of umbrellas, you could choose not to expose your dog to them. If the fear relates to vacuums, brooms or mops, shut your dog in a 'safe room' when you clean the house. Most of the time it is not as simple as avoiding the trigger and you need to find a way to reduce your dog's fear permanently.

Once again, do not try to comfort your dog when it shows signs of fear. This only serves to reinforce to your dog that its fearful behaviour is the right way to react. Similarly, do not punish the dog, because this may make the underlying anxiety worse. As with managing noise phobia (described previously), you should teach your dog an appropriate alternative behaviour, such as sitting in a calm, relaxed way, and reward it for this. The training sessions should be held in a safe and quiet environment at least twice a day, if not more. Over time you can start to challenge your dog by exposing it gradually to its fear, such as umbrellas or male people. Eventually the dog will learn that when it is exposed to its fear, if it sits and is calm and relaxed or engages in another behaviour you have taught it, like play, it will receive a treat (see also Desensitisation and Counterconditioning on pages 74 and 75).

If your dog is afraid of going to the veterinary clinic, start by walking past the building only, and reward it if it can do this without showing signs of fear. When the dog is not afraid of walking past the door, try to walk up to the door. Do not enter, but reward the dog when it sits calmly. Next you can try entering the waiting room and just sitting quietly for five to ten minutes at a time. Gradually the dog will learn not to be afraid and that it receives a reward when it sits calmly in the clinic. If you have not yet implemented or taught your dog an alternative enjoyable and appropriate behaviour, you should just ignore any fearful behaviour that your dog displays.

Your veterinarian might prescribe anti-anxiety medication to help your dog to relax. This will increase its concentration and ability to focus on you during the training sessions. Over time you may be able to reduce the dose or even discontinue it.

Sometimes a second, relaxed and easygoing dog can act as a good role model for fearful dogs. This option needs to be thought out carefully, however, because taking on another dog means more time and financial commitments for your family. It also needs to be the right dog. You need a calm dog, which can set a good example, so when the first dog experiences a fearful event, it can look to the more confident dog for guidance as to how it should react.

Dogs with anxiety problems are not normal dogs. Their fear is not rational or appropriate. The aims of the behaviour-modification techniques described here are to reduce the dog's anxiety and to help your dog to fit in more as a member of the family and in day-to-day life. You cannot expect an anxious dog ever to be completely normal, and you need to be committed to a lifelong training program. Routine is the most important thing for a dog with anxiety problems. This means daily exercise, regular meal times and also regular times for training. Having a good understanding of your dog's ways of communicating (see Chapter two) and implementing behaviour modification techniques early will give you the best chance of success.

9:
Abnormal repetitive behaviour

Repetitive actions or behaviour that has no apparent purpose are seen in many animal species, including people and dogs. A person with abnormal repetitive behaviour is said to have obsessive and compulsive disorder (OCD). Affected people can only alleviate their anxiety by performing a certain action over and over again.

Dogs can also exhibit behaviour that serves no purpose or is done over and over again for no reason at all, and this is called a stereotypic or compulsive behaviour. Strictly, such problems in dogs are not referred to as OCD. The repetitive actions might be normal in another situation, like licking or barking, but they become abnormal when the action is repeated with excessive frequency. Other repetitive actions can be abnormal in every situation, like snapping at the air or eating rocks or other unusual objects.

Stereotypic behaviour is one of the most complicated canine problem behaviours to understand. This is because a dog with repetitive behaviour often displays several different problems at the same time. They can also have aggression problems or inappropriate urination. To further complicate things, the signs of repetitive behaviour can be caused by an underlying medical problem, and there may actually be a good reason for your dog's repetitive behaviour. If you suspect that your dog has an abnormal repetitive behaviour problem, it is therefore important to consult your veterinarian for a complete health examination in order to rule out any medical reasons and to confirm your suspicions.

Unfortunately, still not much is known about the causes of repetitive behaviour. People have noted, however, that certain repetitive behaviours are seen in some breeds more than others, which means that genetics is likely to play a role. Similarly, the age at which dogs can develop repetitive behaviour problems is not known, but it is most commonly seen in young, healthy dogs. As with many types of behaviour problems, you will have the best chance of fixing the problem and helping your dog if you are able to recognise the signs early and to intervene appropriately.

It is important to understand the difference between normal and abnormal repetitive behaviour. The first has a reason behind it, while the second occurs for no apparent reason. This can be very confusing, because the same repetitive behaviour could be considered normal in one dog but abnormal in another. For example, licking is a common repetitive behaviour. A dog may lick constantly at its paws because they are itchy due to a skin condition. This is considered normal, because the repetitive behaviour has a purpose—it alleviates the dog's itchy feet. Another dog may lick constantly at its paws, even though they are not itchy, sore or dirty. This repetitive behaviour is considered abnormal.

Every time your dog exhibits repetitive behaviour, you need to think carefully and look closely to see if there might be a reason for the behaviour. This is not always easy to identify so you will need to consult with your veterinarian or a veterinary behaviour specialist.

You need to be aware that all types of repetitive behaviour can be a means of seeking your attention, and an underlying anxiety disorder can lead to this. Some dogs need or want more attention than others and can be particularly clever at finding means of receiving it. This is sometimes how a repetitive behaviour starts. You may have inadvertently laughed or patted your dog when it was chasing its tail, howling or snapping at a fly for example. Next time your dog wants some attention, and leaning on you or barking is not working, it might start to chase its tail, howl or snap at the air again. Over time your dog may repeat the same action just to provoke a response (see Chapter five).

One way to help to determine if your dog is seeking attention is to monitor what your dog does when no one is at home. You can do this by setting up a tape recorder or a camera. If there is nobody around, your attention-seeking dog is not likely to try the repetitive behaviour as much, if at all. If the behaviour continues even when nobody is around, attention-seeking is unlikely to be the underlying cause of it.

The first stage of managing a dog with attention-seeking repetitive behaviour is to remove all forms of attention you give the dog while the repetitive behaviour is happening. Do not even look at your dog, talk to it, touch it, yell at it or acknowledge your dog at all while it is performing the repetitive behaviour. This can be very challenging, especially for the first few times the behaviour occurs, and you should be prepared for the behaviour to become worse for a short time before it becomes any better. It is particularly hard if the behaviour is noisy or annoying, but you must be strict in order to achieve results.

It is critical to combine this method of ignoring the undesirable behaviour with giving attention when your dog is quiet and calm. Positive reinforcement can be easy to forget, but it is very important. To reward your dog's calm and quiet behaviour you can play with it or groom it, or you can pat and speak to your dog quietly. This combination teaches your dog that it only receives the attention it wants when it is calm and quiet. For more information on attention-seeking problems, refer to Attention seeking behaviour on page 99. If you are using these simple management strategies correctly and they do not work, then attention seeking may not be the reason for your dog's repetitive behaviour.

Boredom is commonly used as an excuse for repetitive behaviour, such as a dog chasing its tail or snapping at the air. In fact, boredom is very rarely associated with repetitive behaviour. Boredom is also one of the easiest possible reasons to rule out. If you provide your dog with adequate exercise, a selection of toys, a change of scenery every now and then, and some time to interact with people, it will not be bored. If your dog continues to exhibit repetitive behaviour, boredom is not the cause.

Anxiety can be an underlying issue in many different behaviour problems, including repetitive behaviour. Sometimes the anxiety can come from a past experience, like a fearful event or an injury. In this case, every time the dog is reminded of the event, by bumping or even looking at the previously injured area, it may become extremely anxious and start chewing or licking at the area. Also, certain objects or noises may have a similar effect. For example, some dogs are frightened by children. Children can be unpredictable and make sounds that are loud and quite strange to a dog. If your dog has been frightened by children in the past, every time it sees or hears children, it may become anxious.

You may be able to avoid the things that you know make your dog anxious, but sometimes the cause for the anxiety cannot be identified. You cannot expect to manage or alleviate repetitive behaviour without addressing the underlying anxiety. This is discussed further in Chapter eight. In addition, you should take your dog to your veterinarian for a complete health check and for guidance in managing the anxiety problem.

Any illness can cause your dog to act in an apparently abnormal way. Specific examples of illnesses and the repetitive behaviours they may initiate are listed in the following sections.

Eating abnormal objects

The act of eating abnormal objects is called pica. Pica commonly occurs in puppies, and most of the time it is caused by natural curiosity rather than being an abnormal repetitive behaviour. Puppies commonly chew on socks or eat rocks and bark. They also might eat their own stools or those of other animals such as cats, rabbits or horses. Eating foreign objects can be extremely serious, because the object can become stuck in the food pipe, stomach or the intestines, and this can be life-threatening. On one occasion, we treated a Labrador Retriever puppy that loved to chew and swallow rocks. He vomited one of the rocks and managed to inhale it into his airway. This blocked his airway, causing him to suffocate and turn blue, and he required emergency treatment to retrieve the rock.

Generally owners discourage puppies from eating random objects, so the puppy learns not to eat the wrong things and will usually grow out of it. Prevent your puppy access to such items while it is learning. You may need to puppy-proof your home, by moving the cat litter tray, fencing off areas with pebbles or ensuring socks are always out of reach. Taking actions like this could save your puppy's life. You need to teach your puppy what it is allowed to chew on by supplying it with a safer alternative. Robust toys and ice cubes work well. You should distract your puppy as soon as it picks up a strange object to chew, and replace the object with the ice cube or play toy. Praise the puppy when it takes the right toy.

Occasionally pica can continue into adulthood, or become apparent for the first time in an adult dog. Sometimes there is a valid reason to explain why your dog is eating unusual objects. Sometimes an underlying anxiety issue drives this behaviour.

The strange items that dogs eat vary, but truly abnormal dogs with pica usually seek out the same object over and over again. One of the more common items that dogs seek out to eat is animal stools. As you can understand, this is a particularly anti-social behaviour and makes that doggy breath even more unpleasant! However, there are many reasons why normal dogs might eat stools. Firstly, it is hard for people to appreciate, but important to know, that some dogs find the smell of certain types of stools particularly inviting. Indeed, our own dog Milo seems to have a particular desire to eat both cat and horse stools with a disturbingly ferocious appetite. Every time he can access these types of stool, his behaviour and desire is reinforced by the immediate 'food' reward. For this reason it is impossible to call him away from the cat's litter tray once he starts eating; the only way we can manage this problem is to prevent possible access to stools at all. Luckily, our cat Beetle also finds the behaviour disturbing and has obliged by learning to toilet outside, where he will not be disturbed. Although it does not make it easier to manage, dogs that eat other species' stools are probably normal.

Some conditions can cause a dog to become constantly hungry, and the dog may eat stools simply to satisfy its ravenous appetite. A lack of digestive enzymes, which occurs in some pancreatic diseases, intestinal worm infestations, inflammatory bowel disease (IBD), some hormonal diseases and even with some medications, can cause a dog to be hungry constantly. Dogs with dietary deficiencies, such as iron deficiency, may actively seek out and eat their own stools, dirt or clay in an attempt to obtain certain nutrients. Because good-quality dog food is so affordable these days, it is rare to find a dog with an incomplete diet. It is more likely that a dog with a nutrient deficiency has a medical problem related to the digestive system, which means it is unable to digest or absorb nutrients through its intestines. It is important to take your dog to your veterinarian for a full examination to rule out these other diseases as a cause for your dog wanting to eat stools.

Dogs with true pica are generally healthy, have a well-balanced diet and are not hungry all the time. They will also frequently strain in order to go to the toilet just so they can eat their stools immediately after. There are some products on the market that you can feed your dog to make its stools smell even more unpleasant than normal, and these act to deter your dog from eating it. Another option is to spray or pour a bitter-tasting substance over the stools. Such products may be available from your local veterinarian or pet store. Both these methods need to be combined with praise for the dog when it leaves its stools alone. If nothing will deter your dog from eating its stools then preventing exposure to stools is the only other option. This means you need to pick up the stools several times a day, immediately after they are produced, if possible.

Most dogs at some stage in their life will eat grass and this is often a cause of concern for many dog owners. There are many theories as to why dogs eat grass and these are discussed in Chapter seven. It may be completely normal for your dog to eat grass from time to time.

Licking, chewing and self-mutilation

Excessive licking, chewing and other grooming behaviours occur very commonly in dogs, but only a small percentage of those are truly abnormal repetitive behaviours. It may be difficult to differentiate between repetitive behaviours that do and do not have a cause, and your veterinarian may need to do several tests and trial certain medications to determine if there is an underlying cause for the excessive licking or chewing.

Excessive licking and chewing are often associated with skin disease and are rarely a pure behaviour problem. Neurological diseases can also cause the skin to become highly sensitive. Skin allergy is one of the most common reasons why your dog might lick and chew its skin, and it can affect dogs of any age. Allergies may be worse in certain seasons. Fleas are also extremely common in some areas and are around all year long, but are more of a problem in the hot and humid months. Dogs with allergies or fleas may appear normal most of the time, but you may notice that your dog sometimes suddenly jumps up and spins around frantically as if something has bitten it. The dog might chew or lick its skin or scratch. You may not even see any fleas, but some dogs are very sensitive and even just one bite can cause a profound reaction.

Itchy skin is one of the more challenging problems to manage, and it might take several visits to your veterinarian or a specialist veterinary dermatologist before a reason for the excessive licking or scratching can be identified. Excessive licking is a good example of how some repetitive behaviour disorders can have several underlying causes. The behaviour will not be eliminated without investigating all the possibilities and implementing an appropriate treatment plan in consultation with your veterinarian.

A dog wearing an Elizabethan collar.

Compulsive licking that is truly abnormal is often directed towards one particular part of the body, such as the lower limbs. This can lead to what is called a lick granuloma or an acral lick granuloma. This appears as a raised, callous-like red lump on the skin, which the dog licks or chews constantly. Lick granulomas can appear quickly, and your dog may lick intensely at the one spot over and over again until it bleeds. This can go on for weeks.

Treatment options for lick granulomas include applying bitter-tasting ointments to the area or using an Elizabethan head collar (see picture opposite). These approaches may solve the problem initially, but commonly the dog will just direct the licking behaviour to an alternative accessible site, such as another leg, or it may start licking again as soon as these measures are removed. These approaches do not treat the repetitive behaviour itself, but may be necessary in the short term to allow a self-inflicted wound to heal.

Certain types of over-grooming are associated with individual breeds more than others. For example, lick granulomas are most common in labrador retrievers, golden retrievers and german shepherds. Doberman pinschers are more likely than other breeds to suck repeatedly on their flank. Compulsive tail chasing is more common in bull terriers and staffordshire bull terriers than other breeds. Many dogs find it fun to chase their tail, but this becomes destructive and harmful when the behaviour is repetitive, unable to be interrupted and compulsive. Over time the tail might lose hair and wounds may develop where the dog has bitten or held on to it.

These breed-related compulsive behaviours may require more aggressive management and even veterinary medications to help to control the problem, so you should consult a behaviourist, veterinarian or veterinary behaviourist.

Sometimes excessive licking is not directed to the dog's body but towards certain objects or specific surfaces. Some dogs lick rough surfaces, or random objects like the vacuum cleaner or the wall for no apparent reason. Excessive licking of random objects is also a compulsive behaviour and may be managed in the same way as self-mutilation or over-grooming behaviour.

You should check that the object attracting your dog's attention does not smell and is not coated in something that tastes pleasant to your dog. Any of these reasons could explain why the repetitive behaviour occurs.

Other bizarre behaviour

Sometimes dogs act in such bizarre ways that their owners find it difficult to describe them. These behaviours can be due to an underlying neurological disorder or be an unusual repetitive behaviour disorder. Examples include: snapping at the air, walking in circles, staring into space, pacing or twitching. These signs can occur at any age and can vary in frequency from many times a day to once every few weeks. Sometimes the behaviour goes on for hours.

Certain neurological diseases can have signs like these and may be more common in one breed more than others. Cavalier King Charles Spaniels are more likely than many other breeds to develop a disorder where they appear to catch flies. They snap randomly at the air and may be disoriented at the time. This behaviour is most often caused by a mild form of seizure and is often considered a form of mild epilepsy. Sometimes it is very difficult to determine if the repetitive behaviour is occurring for a medical reason or is a compulsive behaviour. Even advanced imaging techniques, like magnetic resonance imaging (MRI) or computed tomography (CT) scans, cannot always determine the cause of neurological diseases. Your veterinarian may recommend various tests and perhaps an anti-epileptic medication to help to manage certain neurological diseases and to determine why your dog is behaving in a strange way.

Helping to reduce repetitive behaviour

There are several general techniques you can use to help dogs with abnormal repetitive behaviour. The first thing you need to do in any situation is to have your dog thoroughly evaluated by your veterinarian. You should provide them with an accurate health history for your dog. The evaluation should include a full physical examination, and your veterinarian may also suggest other tests like taking blood and urine for a general health screen. In many cases this initial evaluation will identify any underlying health problems that explain the abnormal behaviour. Medication or other treatments may be required to manage an underlying disease.

Do not punish your dog when the repetitive behaviour occurs. This is important for several reasons.

Firstly, if the behaviour occurs because your dog is anxious, yelling or physically punishing the dog is likely to make its anxiety worse.

Secondly, if there is an underlying medical reason, like allergic skin disease or neurological disease, no amount of punishment will improve the situation.

Finally, dogs that have no reason at all for their abnormal repetitive behaviour are highly motivated to repeat the behaviour over and over again. No amount of yelling will change that. You may be able to interrupt the behaviour briefly, but the dog is likely to start the behaviour again only a short time later.

Try to identify any stress or a cause for anxiety that may be leading to the repetitive behaviour (see Chapter eight).

Also try to determine if your dog has repetitive behaviour due to attention seeking. If this is the case, the dog generally only shows the behaviour when there are members of the family at home. Using a tape recorder, video camera or webcam when you are out of the house can help to determine this. To address repetitive behaviour due to attention seeking, see page 99.

If attention seeking is not the cause for the repetitive behaviour, then you can use distraction (see Counterconditioning on page 75) to try to stop your dog's unwanted behaviour. You are most likely to be successful if distraction is used as soon you see the repetitive behaviour starting to emerge. Instead of giving the dog food as a distraction to stop the behaviour, use another mechanism like spraying it with a water jet, calling it or showing it a toy or food treat. Only after your dog sits and is calm, should you reward this good behaviour. If you give the reward too early or before the dog has stopped the behaviour, you are inadvertently encouraging the repetitive behaviour.

In the first few weeks of training, many dogs will not stop the repetitive behaviour for anything. This is because the dog finds satisfaction in performing it. So you need to spend extra time with your dog when it is not exhibiting the strange behaviour to teach it how to be relaxed and respond to you. Being diligent in basic training will enable you to call your dog to you even in the face of distraction (see Basic training techniques, page 51).

Dogs thrive on routine with regular exercise and regular meal times. In a household with a regular routine, the dog knows what to expect during the day and is generally much happier because of this. Encourage your dog to be relaxed, by talking calmly to it at all times, as this helps it to become a much better adjusted member of the pack. You should not encourage over-excited behaviour or pay too much attention to the dog when you first arrive home. Reward your dog with patting and food when it is lying calmly.

Repetitive behaviour is certainly one of the most complicated behaviour problems in dogs. It is impossible to cover every variation or type of repetitive behaviour in this book, and the examples listed here are generalised, so they may not apply to your dog exactly. You will need to speak to a behaviourist, veterinarian or veterinary behaviourist about your individual dog for more specific solutions. Sometimes behaviour modification is impossible to achieve without short-term medication. Over time many dogs can be weaned off this, as long as the behaviour-modification techniques are continued.

10:
Canine aggression

One of the most common and serious canine behaviour problems is aggression. As with any behaviour problem or medical condition, prevention is ideal, but the next best thing is early identification and intervention to stop the problem progressing. Aggressive dogs are difficult to manage, but with understanding, patience and appropriate communication skills, most types of aggression can be well controlled. Because canine aggression problems are so serious, it is important to involve a behaviourist, veterinarian or veterinary behaviourist in the treatment. In serious cases medication may be required.

Aggressive dogs are not simply badly behaved or naughty, they respond to certain situations in an abnormal way. This is in contrast to aggression exhibited by a normal dog when there is an underlying reason such as pain. With the exception of abuse or neglect, problem aggression is rarely caused by people. However, people can unintentionally make aggression worse if they do not handle aggressive dogs appropriately.

> Canine aggression problems are serious. You should seek professional advice if your dog has an aggression problem.

Aggression problems can be a serious issue for other people and animals in the dog's family or pack, as well as for anyone else coming in contact with the dog, including visitors, members of the public, groomers, veterinarians and other dogs. In general, an aggressive dog does not fit in easily as a pack member, and more time and effort must be taken to make the dog more socially acceptable.

A common consequence of canine aggression is dog-fight wounds. Dogs can cause serious harm, especially when the victim is smaller or weaker than the attacker. In many cases wounds are superficial and minor, but they can be life threatening, needing immediate emergency treatment and can lead to permanent disability. Aggressive dogs are difficult for veterinarians to treat. Sometimes it is difficult to perform a simple examination, let alone treat a health problem.

Some people believe that certain breeds of dog are aggressive. Actually, while genes do play a part in a dog's nature, in many cases management and environment play a bigger role. We have met many pit bull terrier dogs who would not hurt a fly, and many 80-kilogram rottweilers and mastiffs who just want a cuddle. These dogs have great natures, are well adjusted and have been handled well by their owner. It certainly is not just big dogs that are aggressive.

The worst bites we have received have been from a jack russell terrier and a basenji. Some individual dogs simply are aggressive by nature.

Aggression problems are not created overnight, instead they tend to escalate with time if left unmanaged. For this reason, it is vital that you know how to recognise the first signs. These can appear at any age, but are most often noticed when the dog reaches social maturity, usually at about 18 to 24 months of age, but sometimes slightly earlier or later.

Dogs can become aggressive for a number of reasons and in a variety of situations. In many cases it is an exaggerated normal response to a particular event. For example, an owner might consider it normal for a dog to bark or growl if a stranger enters the house or yard uninvited. This behaviour becomes unwanted or abnormal when the aggression cannot be controlled, and the dog might start to growl, bark at or even bite invited guests, despite the owner being present and trying to stop the dog. Another example is when a dog growls or bites another animal or person if they try to remove its food. This is common in the wild if food is scarce, but aggression like this is unacceptable in the home, and, as the leader of the dog's pack, the owner should always be able to remove and return the dog's food bowl easily and without fear of the dog becoming aggressive.

There are numerous causes of aggression and identifying these can be very difficult. Some episodes may be related to a bad experience early in the dog's life associated with fear and anxiety. At other times a dog may be fiercely protective of a certain toy or a member of the family. Other dogs might be aggressive in random situations and are unpredictable. Aggression problems often start small, but they can gradually escalate until they cause a major problem. It is amazing what some people will put up with when it comes to their dog. In extreme cases owners may be forced to sleep on the couch, because the dog will growl and attack them when they try to sleep in the bed or move the dog off the bed. A dog that scares its owner does not make a good family pet.

Canine aggression is a complex problem, and no one dog can be managed in exactly the same way as another. It would also be wishful thinking to believe that all aggressive dogs can be cured or that all aggression problems can be prevented. However, we strongly believe that if armed with the language of canine communication and if working in association with your behaviourist, veterinarian or veterinary behaviourist, you can help to prevent aggression or manage an aggressive dog, particularly if you intervene early.

Prevention

Some aspects of how to prevent behaviour problems are discussed in Chapter three. However, it is important to highlight a few key points that relate particularly to aggression. Prevention starts the very first day you buy a new dog. In fact, it starts before you buy your new dog. Choosing the right dog that suits your lifestyle is the first step. For example, housing an energetic working dog such as a kelpie or border collie in a small yard, or being unable to walk a dog of this breed at least twice a day is likely to lead to the dog being bored and having excess energy. Sometimes a dog might express its frustration and spend that excess energy by destroying the garden or tearing the washing off the clothesline. Other dogs respond by being aggressive.

Most dogs join their new pack, your family, at an early age. The puppy's first three to four months, when it is developing, are when it is most receptive to learning and accepting of new experiences. During this period the puppy learns how to interact with other dogs and people, and it learns to accept things in its environment. It is vital to expose the puppy to as many positive experiences as possible and give it praise and positive reinforcement when it behaves well. Encouragement is a much more successful training tool than punishment.

Obedience training should start early. Training helps you to develop a relationship with your puppy, and the early warning signs of aggression are easy to identify when you have a good relationship with your dog and when you understand how to communicate. Dogs are like children, they need guidance to know what is allowed and what is not allowed. Dogs, especially more dominant dogs, will push the boundaries unless they are taught the correct behaviour. If inappropriate behaviour is allowed to develop, it is much more difficult to correct later in life.

One of the important lessons you can teach your young puppy is that it cannot bite hands, feet or any part of a person. This is called mouthing. Most pups will mouth at some stage and this is a normal part of play and curiosity. Encouraging your young dog to play with your feet might be fun when it is ten weeks old, but it should not be allowed to grow into an adult dog with adult teeth that still thinks mouthing or biting people is acceptable behaviour. When the puppy starts to mouth a person's feet or hands, you should offer it a suitable chew toy instead.

Another serious form of aggression that you need to identify and correct early is food-related aggression. Any signs of aggression over food or treats, such as staring, growling and baring teeth, should be discouraged with a sharp 'No!' The puppy must then earn back the reward. Teach the puppy that it must sit and wait for you, the leader of the pack, to tell it that it can have the treat. The puppy will soon learn that by sitting and behaving well, it receives the food reward. You should aim to be able to take food and treats away from the puppy easily and return them straight away to the puppy without any signs of aggression.

A normal puppy should learn this quickly. If the puppy continues to show signs of aggression despite simple training steps, it is a sign that professional guidance is needed to prevent a problem developing. Unfortunately, in many cases problems are only addressed after the best period for learning has passed. Once the dog reaches physical maturity, the aggression can become quite dangerous.

Aggression can be divided into general groups based on the reasons for aggression. Aggressive dogs display certain traits that can help to tell us what type they have and so why they behave aggressively. The different types of aggression should be addressed in different ways. The next section will describe the traits of the most common types of aggression and how you can communicate with your dog in order to help to reduce the problem.

Fear aggression

This is one of the most common types of aggression and can be directed towards other dogs or people. In most cases the dog becomes scared or threatened in the face of fairly normal situations or experiences. For example, it might be afraid of a stranger greeting it in the street or other dogs in the dog park. Sometimes it might be afraid of a certain noise such as the kettle boiling and react in an abnormal way for no apparent reason. It may also be overly frightened when it is examined by a veterinarian.

Fear can start after a traumatic event early in the dog's life, such as a stranger popping a balloon. The dog might start to think that every new person it meets is going to make the same frightening sound. A normal dog will learn that new people are, in general, fun, non-threatening and do not make frightening noises. Some dogs become so afraid that they become aggressive in order to protect themselves from perceived harm. Fear can also start after a painful experience. For example, some dogs will remember the pain from an ear infection and anticipate that each time its ears are touched, the pain will return. Over time this may escalate to the point where the dog becomes aggressive when anyone tries to pat it on the head.

It is easy to understand that a dog that is the victim of abuse is much more likely to develop fear aggression. In a similar way, if a dog is physically punished inappropriately, then it may learn to fear the person rather than to associate the punishment with the bad behaviour. Over time the dog will hide from the person or people in general, and, if the fear becomes too great, the dog may become aggressive.

Fear aggression can develop at any age, but most commonly the first signs can be seen early, before the onset of social maturity, around 18 to 24 months of age. Unfortunately, it is not always easy to identify a reason why a dog should be afraid.

A dog suffering from fear aggression has recognisable body language. Its body will tend to be crouched low, its head will be held low with its ears back, and it may sometimes tremble and hold its tail between its legs while barking or growling. A dog with fear aggression will bark and vocalise more than dogs with other types of aggression. The most common sequence of events is that the dog will bark, growl and back away from the fear, then may snap and bite as a last resort, if it feels cornered and the perceived threat becomes too great. A normal dog in comparison might also have its tail between its legs and ears back when it is afraid, and it might also tremble and back away to hide, but it will not show any signs of aggression and may roll over and show its belly as a submissive posture.

Reducing fear aggression

You should not corner a dog with fear aggression. The priority of a fearful dog is to run or hide from a threat. If it is cornered, it will feel trapped and might growl or bite, because it no longer has an escape route.

It is common for an owner to react by trying to comfort the dog with reassuring words and pats. People naturally want to reassure the dog that it is alright and that it does not need to be fearful. This is actually one of the worst things to do, because you are telling the dog that it is okay to be fearful and to react an aggressive way. This makes it more likely to respond in the same way, if not worse, the next time it experiences a fearful event.

Also do not use physical punishment to discipline a fearful dog. Even a sharp tap on the nose or on the bottom can make its fear worse or elicit an aggressive retaliation.

When you are training a fearful dog, try to reward only good calm and relaxed behaviour, not fearful behaviour. As with any behaviour problem, it is better if you can detect and address fear aggression as soon as it starts to emerge. If a dog is becoming frightened it may become alert, then its pupils may grow large. Its tail will be tucked between its legs, and it may then start growling, which is usually the first sign of aggression before any overt biting. If you can identify these initial stages, you have a much better chance of stopping them progressing.

Try to distract your dog as soon as you see any signs of inappropriate behaviour. For example, if the dog is growling at a new person visiting the home, call it away, ask it to sit calmly and use food and praise or play as a reward for the good behaviour. If you need more control, you could attach a long lead to the dog's collar at all times. If you cannot distract your dog or call it away, you can then gently pull it away with the lead. Once you have its attention, ask it to sit and stay for a reward. If the dog does not respond to you or food rewards and continues to show signs of fear aggression, remove it from the fearful stimulus entirely. Only once it sits and stays in a calm, relaxed manner can you reward it.

Fearful dogs need more security than other dogs, so, as with other behaviour problems, you should try to establish a regular routine and a clear hierarchy within the household. A regular walking time and feeding time can be very beneficial. To help your dog know where it fits into the pack, spend some time with your dog every day to practise simple training commands. Once these basic training commands can be performed easily in an environment without distractions, you can start to practise them in progressively more challenging situations. Ultimately you will find it much easier to distract your dog and call it away from a situation in which it is fearful.

Early on in the training process you should try to avoid any fearful events. For example, if the dog is afraid of new dogs, do not go straight to the dog park and avoid walking close to other dogs on the street. Every time a dog with fear aggression is exposed to its fear, the inappropriate and aggressive reaction is reinforced. Increase the dog's exposure to the fearful event gradually. Introduce a new dog at a distance first; pick a friendly dog, but not one that is too excitable. If your dog behaves well you can reward it. Over time you can start bringing the other dog gradually closer. If your dog shows any signs of fear aggression, take it away from the other dog, make it sit calmly and only then give it a reward. You can then start the process again at the last distance that it would tolerate the other dog while remaining calm and relaxed.

Many fear aggressive dogs improve with training, but fearful dogs will never be fully cured of their problem, so you will have to continue a maintenance behaviour-modification program for life. Sometimes only a slight improvement is needed for the dog to become a welcome and socially acceptable member of the family again.

Food-related aggression

In the wild, dogs had to protect any food they obtained from other competing dogs, sometimes in order to survive. Even in a domestic situation where food may not be restricted and the environment is less competitive, this instinct persists.

It is more apparent in some dogs than others and can turn into food-related aggression. The aggression can be directed towards people, dogs or both. The aggression often becomes worse if the food is highly prized. For example, a dog with food-related aggression might growl and show its teeth if someone approaches while it is eating canned dog food, but it might lunge and bite if it is eating treats such as raw hides, pig's ears or bones. Such treats are classic triggers for food-related aggression.

Food-related aggression is commonly first seen in early puppyhood. The puppy might snap at other dogs while eating or not allow a treat to be removed without biting the owner. It is important to recognise these early signs. Food-related aggression can be corrected as long as it is noticed early and addressed quickly. If it is not recognised and there is no intervention, then it is likely to worsen as the puppy matures. There is also a possibility that food-related aggression may be an early sign of dominance aggression (see Dominance aggression on page 135). Not all puppies with food-related aggression will develop dominance aggression, but dominance aggression can be serious and tends to worsen over time, so it is critical to intervene early.

Reducing food-related aggression

Once food-related aggression is established, it can be one of the most difficult forms of aggression to correct. However, food-related aggression is also one of the easiest forms of aggression to avoid. Be observant when your dog is eating, and watch what it does when you enter the room or when you approach it. Also watch how your dog reacts to other dogs while it is eating. Look for staring, curling of the lips and growling. If you can recognise these early-warning signs, then you can implement strategies to prevent the problem progressing.

Teach your puppy from the start that it has to sit and wait for its food. This means that it has to submit to you; you are feeding the puppy on your terms, not on its terms. You should also teach it to give up its food bowl even if there is food in it. To do this, try first to remove the empty food bowl and give it back immediately with a treat in the bowl if your puppy allows this with no signs of aggression. This teaches your puppy that if it allows its bowl to be removed, it is replaced straight away with a greater reward. You can then try giving your puppy a small amount of food, then remove it while it is still eating. If the puppy allows you to do this, replace it quickly with a larger amount of food or a tastier food treat. These techniques will teach your puppy that it will not always lose the food when you remove it, and, in fact, if it does not react, it will ultimately receive a greater food reward. Practising this may be the only way to detect the early signs of food-related aggression.

Continue this training process throughout your dog's life. This reminds your dog that it must allow you to remove food at your will. If you can safely remove food from your dog, you can also remove potentially harmful objects or rotten food it might pick up in the street. For example, our own dog, Milo is very clever at picking up discarded barbequed chicken bones off the street when we are out walking. Such scavenging is potentially dangerous. Fortunately, we have trained Milo to allow us to remove anything from his mouth without a problem. If a dog has food-related aggression, you might not be able to do this safely.

If your dog is aggressive when eating, start by teaching it to sit and wait calmly before it is given food. Initially use a bowl to offer your dog small portions at a time. This is safer than hand feeding it. Once your dog can be fed from a bowl with no signs of aggression, you can start to ask it to sit and wait calmly and feed it small amounts from an open hand. Once it is able to do this with no signs of aggression, you can then start to try to remove its food bowl. Divide its normal meal into small portions, then feed it one of these portions. Once that portion of food is finished, carefully remove the bowl and replace it immediately with the second portion of food. If the dog is progressing, it will eventually learn that if it allows the bowl to be removed, it will be replaced with more food. In due course you can progress to removing the dog's food bowl while it is still eating. If it gives it up with no signs of aggression, you can immediately replace it with more food or a tasty treat and verbally praise it. Of course you need to be careful not to increase your dog's overall ration, as this could lead to obesity and related health problems.

In some cases, the aggression cannot be corrected even with the guidelines outlined above and the dog may never be able to be trusted when eating. In these cases, it is best to avoid every potential conflict. Do not place your hand in or near the food bowl when the dog is eating. Do not tease the dog with food, and do not allow children to walk around with food in their hands when the dog is present.

Avoid giving your dog food treats altogether, especially raw hides, pig's ears and bones. This might sound cruel, but by avoiding the associated aggression, both you and your dog are less distressed and safer. If you especially wish to give your dog a treat, leave it on the floor or in its bowl for it to find, rather than giving it to it by hand. Allow your dog to eat the treat in a closed room away from people or other dogs. There is always a risk that the dog will bury or hide the treat. If this occurs, it may uncover the treat at a later date and become aggressive to other dogs or people nearby at the time.

If you have more than one dog and one, or both, has food-related aggression, do not feed them together. Allowing the dogs to eat together will give the aggressive dog the opportunity to growl or bite at the other dog, which acts as a form of positive reinforcement. You should never interpose yourself between two dogs that are aggressive over food as this can be very dangerous.

Dominance aggression

Dominance is a term used to describe a dog that tends to want or need to be in control. It is important to understand that dominant behaviour is a natural aspect of normal canine behaviour (see Chapter two) and the pack hierarchical structure (see Chapter one). In contrast, dominance aggression is an abnormal behaviour problem, in which a dog uses aggression to gain control of a situation. Normal dogs that are naturally dominant use other tricks to gain control, like pushing on you, jumping up at you and pulling on the lead. Dominance aggression is one of the most complex forms of aggression because it can appear very variable. Dogs with dominance aggression can also have food-related aggression, territorial aggression, protective aggression or possessive aggression.

You might wonder why it is such a problem to allow your family dog to become the leader of the pack. You may think that if the dog is happy to be leader, and wants to be in control, then why not let it? Well, it will lead to many problems. Firstly, a dominant dog that is allowed to be in control will challenge the members of the family in order to assert itself. For example, a dominant dog might determine that it needs to be in control of the couch. If anyone tries to remove the dog from the couch or even sit on the couch, they are likely to be met with resistance and possibly aggression. This is just the dog's way of communicating that it has control and can dictate who sits on 'its' couch. Furthermore, if it learns that this type of behaviour is acceptable, it reinforces the aggressive dominant behaviour. This supports the dog's idea that it is head of the pack. This is how dominance can turn into dominant aggression.

People may worry that a dog will be unhappy if it is treated as the lowest member of the pack. This is not true. Every dog is content and at its most relaxed when it knows its position in the hierarchy. Even dominant dogs are happy to be led by a master. However, a dominant dog needs a stronger leader than a dog that is more submissive.

The first signs of dominance aggression most often occur at the onset of social maturity, which is at about 18 to 24 months of age, but can occur slightly earlier or later. Dominance aggression usually progresses over time and is much more common in male dogs than female dogs. Initially the signs of dominance aggression may be subtle and go unnoticed. If left unchecked, the behaviour can progress very quickly, and the dog may eventually bite a family member for challenging its rank or status.

Another scenario where dominance aggression may occur is when people notice growling or snarling at a new baby or new dog. The assumption that the dog is jealous of the attention the new family member is receiving is not always true. Often, your dog simply views the new member as a threat to its position in the hierarchy. Once again, if the early warning signs of dominance aggression are not identified, it may seem like the dog is becoming aggressive suddenly or for no reason. Early intervention and effective management of dominant dogs is vital and can help to prevent aggression.

Dominant dogs display certain characteristics that you need to watch for (also see Chapter two). These include leaning on people, straddling or standing over people, blocking doorways, staring and 'talking back'. It can also include what might be seen as hugs and kisses, where a dog might place its paws on your shoulders and lick your face. This might seem loving and cute, but allowing your dog to do this gives it the message that you are submitting to its dominance. If you identify some of these characteristics in your dog, you need to be aware that it has a tendency to be dominant. It does not mean that it will become aggressive, but you should actively discourage the dominant behaviour to help to stop it from progressing to aggression. See the rank reduction program on page 12 for ways to regain or maintain your position as leader of the pack.

A dominant dog might interpret some of the normal ways people interact as being a challenge. For example, staring at a dog, handling its head or muzzle, leaning over it, putting on a leash, stepping over it or pushing on its rump, bathing or grooming or handling its paws to cut its nails can all be interpreted as a challenge to the dog's dominance. A dog with dominance aggression may respond by growling, snarling and bearing its teeth, snapping or biting. It may also respond aggressively to any discipline or punishment.

In some cases, a dog behaves in a dominant way in order to attract attention. This may be an indication of underlying anxiety and is different to a dominant dog that simply desires to be in control. Anxious dogs often are very needy and require a lot of attention. An anxious dog may learn that being pushy is the most effective way to gain attention. For example, dominant behaviour such as nudging or pawing at someone's arms or legs attracts attention (see Chapter eight). In any case, dominant behaviour needs to be identified and managed early to prevent it from progressing to dominance aggression.

Reducing dominance aggression

Becoming a strong leader and encouraging every member of the family to do the same, is one of the most important things that you can do to help to manage a dog with dominance aggression. This starts with basic training as a puppy and continues throughout the dog's life.

A strong leader gives clear messages to the dog, praises the dog for appropriate behaviour and does not allow the dog to have control. Every member of the family needs to help to train the dog, including children. This will help the dominant dog to learn that it needs to take its cues from every member of the family and not just one person in charge of training. Tell children to ask the dog to sit before feeding it. Involve them in training sessions, and teach them how to be safe around the dog.

A strong leader also constantly reinforces their position as the leader of the pack and the dog's position as subordinate. To do this you can:

• Always ask your dog to sit and wait calmly and in a relaxed way for attention, play, praise, toys or food.

- Walk through doorways before the dog, asking the dog to wait at the door, then calling it through once you have entered.
- Feed the dog last—in the wild, the head of the pack always has the first choice of the food and the lowest member eats last.
- And use a Rank Reduction Program (see Chapter one) for additional ways to regain or maintain your position as leader of the pack.

Desexing your dog can help. Hormones play a role in aggression, and removing those hormones can have several positive effects. You should be aware that neutering or desexing does not always prevent or eliminate the problem, as much of the behaviour is learned. However, it usually reduces the frequency and intensity of episodes of dominance aggression. If you are not planning on breeding your dog, we recommend having it neutered or desexed before the onset of sexual maturity, at around six to twelve months.

Consider investing in a head collar rather than using a standard neck collar. It is amazing to see how much more control people have once their dominant dog is properly fitted with a head collar. They are comfortable for the dog and the dog becomes instantly calmer and receives messages more clearly than with a standard lead and collar (see Chapter five). You can even use a head collar on your dog at home. It provides a safe way of doing things such as removing an aggressive dominant dog from the couch.

Regular exercise is an absolute priority. If you have a healthy dog, you should walk it at least once a day. This provides both physical and mental stimulation and helps your dog to relax when it is at home. Your dog will not be so stressed about trying to control every situation when it has spent its spare energy out on a walk. Simply allowing your dog to exercise itself in the yard does not provide enough mental or social stimulation. Regular times for these walks, as well as regular training, meal times and sleep times can be beneficial. Routine helps to reduce anxiety because the dog knows what to expect and when to expect it.

Never challenge a dominantly aggressive dog physically. The dog is likely to become more aggressive to meet your challenge. This only escalates the problem and can be very dangerous. Gradually lowering your dog's rank using a rank reduction program is much safer and more appropriate (see Chapter one: Dogs are pack aimals).

Avoid the situations that trigger the aggression, such as if you step over the dog or handle its paws. This is important because the inappropriate behaviour is reinforced each time an episode occurs. These events can also be dangerous. Once your dog is confident in you as a leader and knows its lower position in the hierarchy, you can more safely interact with your dog.

You should not let your dominant dog sleep on your bed or eat off your plate. Sleeping position is very highly valued in the pack situation. Allowing your dominant dog to sleep in the same place as you gives it the message that you are equal in rank. Similarly food is highly valued amongst dogs and allowing a dominant dog to lick your plate gives it the message that you are of a similar rank in the pack. These simple concessions can inadvertently elevate its position in the hierarchy and can lead to dominance aggression.

Do not allow or encourage your dominant dog to take control of its lead by holding it in its mouth. This may seem entertaining, because it looks like the dog is walking itself, but it may be just another mechanism for a dominant dog to try to control the situation.

Do not play tug-of-war games with a dominant dog. A tug-of-war game is a direct challenge for the dog. If you lose the game, the dog receives the impression that it is stronger and more dominant than you. In fact, even taking on the challenge a dominant dog has set gives the dog the message that it is worthy of your challenge. It is better to just avoid tug-of-war games altogether.

Dogs with dominance aggression can potentially be trained to behave like normal dogs and be acceptable pets. As with every behaviour problem, effective communication with your dog is vital. You must be able to recognise and understand the signs early. You also need to be able to communicate with your dog in a way it can understand. If you allow the dog to win any challenge and be the leader of the pack, you inadvertently reinforce the inappropriate behaviour. Dominant dogs will always be that way by nature and will continue to challenge for control and push the limits. For this reason, managing and training a dominant dog or a dog with dominance aggression never ends. Training does not cure the problem, but helps to manage it so that the dog and the family can live in harmony.

Interdog aggression

Aggression can be directed towards dogs within the same household, dogs outside the household or both. The aggression may occur whenever the dog encounters another dog, or it may occur only in specific situations. It can be very difficult to differentiate genuine interdog aggression from some of the other forms of aggression, such as fear, food-related dominance or territorial aggression. While some cases are obvious, many dogs have multiple forms of aggression, so they can be challenging to classify.

Dogs with interdog aggression are not normally aggressive towards people. They commonly misinterpret the body language of other dogs as being threatening and respond by becoming aggressive towards them. Most dogs with interdog aggression have an underlying anxiety problem, which makes them react in an abnormal aggressive way (see Chapter eight: Canine anxiety). They cope with this anxiety by being aggressive. This may seem strange, but remember dogs do not experience emotions like people and they communicate their anxiety in very different ways.

Interdog aggression most commonly develops first at the onset of social maturity, at about 18 to 24 months of age, but can occur slightly earlier or later. A common scenario is that two dogs have been living in harmony for one or two years, then suddenly they start to fight. Once one or both of the dogs reach social maturity, they may begin to challenge each other's position in the hierarchy and fight until that hierarchy is re-established, probably with the younger or fitter dog at the top.

When the aggression is directed towards dogs outside of the household, anxiety is once again commonly the underlying problem. When two dogs meet for the first time, they establish a hierarchy within a very short period of time, if not instantly. They use body language to communicate if they are dominant and in control or if they are more submissive (see Chapter two: illustrations on pages 23, 26 and 30). Most dogs find the signals easy to read. Normal dogs understand that another dog with its tail held high and wagging freely wants to interact and has friendly intentions, whereas another dog that stares intently with its hair standing on end does not. Dogs with interdog aggression are not good at reading these signals, are anxious about where they stand in the hierarchy and use aggression in order to establish this.

Reducing interdog aggression

Initially you should try to avoid potential triggers for interdog aggression. Do not let your dog loose in the park or do not leave your two dogs at home alone unattended. If your dog tries to attack a particular dog every time you walk it, take a different route or go at a different time to help to avoid it. Each of these situations could lead to dog fights, and dog fight wounds can be serious and require veterinary attention. Also whenever your dog exhibits interdog aggression the behaviour is reinforced, which makes the problem worse.

To reduce your dog's aggression, spend some time practising basic training exercises with it every day. Work up to a point where the dog will sit and stay calmly in both quiet situations and situations where there are more distractions. Only when you achieve good voice control in the presence of noise and other distractions can you try to introduce your dog to new canine friends while on the lead.

Consider using a head collar during the training process. This can be important because dogs with interdog aggression may not be as good at picking up and understanding signals. A head collar can also make it much easier to lead the dog away from a potentially aggressive situation should it occur during the training process, on the street or in the park.

Once you have good voice control over your dog, you can start to desensitise your dog to other dogs (see Fear aggression on page 128). Gradually the dog will react less and less to the sight of other dogs and learn that it only receives praise and rewards when it sits calmly.

Conflicts tend to occur between dogs of similar rank, and this can be exacerbated if one dog has just reached social maturity. You can make the situation worse if you treat the two dogs as equals. You can also make the situation worse by favouring the lower ranking dog and inadvertently raising its rank, perhaps because you feel sorry for it. First you need to determine which is the naturally more dominant dog and most able to maintain its position in the hierarchy without your help. Most commonly this is the younger, stronger, fitter dog, but this depends heavily on your individual situation.

You then need to deliberately lower the rank of the naturally more submissive dog (see Rank Reduction Program on page 15). This results in a separation of the dogs' ranks, which ultimately means less conflict and a more harmonious pack. For you to be able to do this both dogs need to view you as the ultimate leader and top of the hierarchy.

The rank reduction program involves ensuring the more dominant dog has access to everything before the other dog. This includes food, treats, having the leash put on and play. If it is not safe to let the dogs be alone together, lock them up in separate rooms when you are out but allow the younger, fitter dog to have the best room. It may also be beneficial to neuter the lower ranking dog, if not both of them. These measures may seem cruel to the older or weaker dog, but in fact both dogs will be calmer and happier.

Play aggression

It is normal for dogs to play. Dogs play with other dogs, people and sometimes other animals such as cats. Dogs play in a variety of ways and can make quite a vast array of play noises! A play growl or bark usually has a higher pitch, and the dog might bark quickly and frequently. It is not normal for dogs to become aggressive when they play. Dogs with play aggression might growl and raise the hair on their backs when they start to play.

Play aggression may occur if a puppy was not taught appropriate ways to play. In most situations, puppies learn to play politely with their littermates. They learn quickly what is acceptable, as the other pups or the mother discipline the puppy if it is playing too roughly. If a puppy is removed from its litter too early or it is raised in an environment where rough play is encouraged, it may never have the opportunity to learn what is appropriate and what is not.

Reducing play aggression

Do not hit the dog if it is being aggressive during a game. The dog will most likely interpret the discipline as another form of play behaviour and this might encourage even more aggressive play.

Do not encourage rough play with a puppy. This includes hitting it around its head or pushing it on its shoulder to instigate play. A dog that was taught to play roughly as a puppy is more likely to extend that rough play into aggression when it becomes an adult dog.

If your dog becomes aggressive when playing, or uses people's hands and feet as play toys, you need to teach it how to play more calmly. Every time your dog becomes aggressive or even shows signs that it might become aggressive, stop the game. This might mean physically leaving the room or saying clearly 'No!' and asking the dog to sit. Conversely you should praise the puppy when it is playing well.

If your dog 'mouths' or uses people's arms or legs as play toys, distract the behaviour by placing a soft toy into the dog's mouth, then continue to encourage normal play behaviour with the toy by praising and patting your dog when it plays with or chews the toy.

Remember that aggressive dogs are not normal dogs. With the exception of abuse or neglect, aggression is not directly caused by people, but people can inadvertently encourage aggression to develop or worsen. To prevent this, you need to understand canine language and understand how your actions might be interpreted by your dog (see Chapter five).

Territorial or protective aggression

Throughout history, people have formed a close bond with their trusted canine companions and have relied on them for protection. Many dogs have a natural instinct to protect and this is stronger in some dogs than in others. It is this instinct that is used when training a dog to be a guard dog. It is important to point out right from the beginning that working guard dogs are highly trained and under complete control. They do not have an aggression problem. They are normal dogs who respond to their trainer's commands. Dogs that have territorial or protective aggression are not normal. They respond to certain situations in an abnormal way and are not under the control of their owners.

Territorial aggression and protective aggression are similar, but not identical, problems. In both types of aggression, the dog identifies something that is very important to it and worthy of protecting. Dogs with territorial aggression typically protect an area of land, a space within the home or even a dog park that they regularly visit. Dogs with protective aggression tend to protect objects, animals or people. In each case the dog may become aggressive towards anyone that it thinks is threatening the object, person or area it needs to protect. Often there is no warning before the aggression is initiated.

You might own or know of a dog that barks or growls at people or other dogs when out for a walk. This can be embarrassing and might seem strange, but might occur because the dog feels that it needs to protect its owner, and does this by growling or biting at the perceived threat. This is not normal behaviour. A normal dog is better at reading the body language and signals of the people or other dogs and also takes cues from its owner if there is a true threat. In the home, a normal dog barks when there is a knock at the door to alert its owner. This is because the dog has learnt to do this by being praised or provoking some reaction from its owner when it has done this in the past. A dog with territorial aggression will bark and growl when there is a knock at the door, but its response may be exaggerated, and it may not stop barking or growling even when instructed to do so.

Dogs can claim anything or any area as being their territory. A common area to protect is the area in or around the home. The territorial response can be exaggerated if the yard is fenced, because the dog knows exactly where its territory ends. It may also be worse when a dog is chained up or caged. Dogs might also protect smaller areas, such as the car, the kennel or the dog's sleeping area. A dog with territorial or protective aggression may bark fiercely if anyone approaches when it is lying in its bed. It perceives anyone, sometimes even its owner, as being a threat to its bed area.

A dog might feel more attached to one member of its pack, or the family, than others. If this situation is extreme, the dog will sometimes bark, growl or even bite another person who tries to hug or show affection to that particular person. The dog may think the other person is threatening its territory.

Territorial or protective aggression usually is first noticed at the onset of social maturity, which occurs at about 18 to 24 months of age, but can occur slightly earlier or later. Dogs with territorial aggression tend not to be aggressive when they are not in their own territory because they do not need to defend it. However, if they frequently visit a particular area, such as a park, they can start to believe that this is their territory. Similarly dogs with protective aggression tend not to be aggressive when the person that they try to protect is not around. Dogs with protective aggression may be more aggressive while on the lead and as soon as they are let off the lead, they no longer feel like they need to protect their owner. You should not use this as a test to try to determine if your dog has protective aggression, but it may be something you have noticed. It is dangerous to have a potentially aggressive dog off the lead and not under your direct control. Typically the intensity of the aggression will grow as the perceived intruder approaches closer to the territory or person the dog is trying to protect.

Reducing territorial or protective aggression

You should never praise aggression. This may seem to be stating the obvious, but people naturally pat and soothe a dog that is distressed and barking. Soothing words and encouragement might work to calm a distressed child, but dogs interpret your signals and actions in very different ways. This can inadvertently give your dog the message that it is acceptable to behave in this way and that you are encouraging it. Instead, you should ask your dog to perform an alternative acceptable behaviour such as sit. If this is not possible, you need to remove your dog from the situation by taking it to another room. The longer the dog is allowed to react without you stopping it, the more likely it is to react in the same way next time.

Discourage your dog from responding to a knock at the door or the ring of the doorbell. Many people worry that if they do not allow the dog to be protective, the dog will not respond if a real threat occurs. This is not the case. Dogs will still react to a real threat situation, because they learn to look to you for guidance. Through practice and training, the dog becomes better at understanding signals from the environment. Also, the aim of training is to teach the dog to take directions from its owner in all circumstances and to listen to its owner as the leader of the pack. If this is effective, then the dog will respond to the owner appropriately in a real threat situation.

Avoid confrontation until the dog has achieved the basics of training. For example, if you know that there will be visitors to the house, lock the dog in another room where it cannot hear the door before the visitors arrive. Only when the atmosphere has settled down should the dog be allowed back into the room where the visitors are. Initially you may have to avoid going to a park that the dog perceives as part of its own territory to avoid a potentially aggressive episode.

Reward your dog when it reacts well. Give your dog treats and praise when it greets the visitors appropriately. Also reward it if it does not overreact to the sound of the door knock or doorbell. Gradually it will associate its calm response to someone coming to the door with rewards.

Try to become a strong leader so that your dog is confident in you as the head of the pack and listens to your instructions (see Chapter one). As with all forms of aggression, go back to the basics. You need to spend at least fifteen minutes every day training your dog, no matter how old it is. Start with 'Sit' and 'Stay' for short periods of time, with no distractions. Gradually build this so you can leave the room, walk away and even perform the commands outside with noise and other distractions. Once you can do this reliably with your dog, you will have a much better chance of teaching it what is and is not appropriate behaviour when there are advances on its territory.

Distract your dog if you can predict an aggressive episode. For example, if you are walking your dog on the lead and see another dog in the distance, attract your dog's attention and ask it to perform a simple command that you have been practising in your training sessions, such as 'Sit'. Always have treats or a toy with you when you go on a walk, so you can reward your dog when it behaves well. Distract your dog until the other dog has passed. Make sure you remember to praise your dog when it does not react to the other dog. This type of training is called counterconditioning (see page 75).

If the dog has a preferred member of the pack, do not give that person all the caring responsibilities, as this will only add to the dog's drive to protect this person. Share the feeding, bathing and walking so all the members of the pack are perceived by the dog as being more equal. By doing this, you will also reinforce the natural hierarchy of the pack, which is that all people, adults and children, are superior to the dog in the pecking order. Dogs feel most relaxed and confident when they have a clear understanding of their position in the pack.

With persistence, patience and consistency, many dogs with territorial or protective aggression will improve. You have the best chance of success when the problem is addressed early. Territorially or protectively aggressive dogs require lifelong maintenance behaviour modification. A lapse from the routine of encouraging good behaviour and discouraging territorial or protective behaviour can result in the dog reverting to the aggressive behaviour you worked so hard to correct.

Maternal aggression

This can occur when a bitch is pregnant, is having a false pregnancy, or after the puppies have been born. Dogs with maternal aggression guard their pups aggressively. A bitch experiencing a false pregnancy may also protect her toys aggressively, as if they were puppies. The bitch will usually warn first by growling and snarling at the perceived threat, such as a person approaching the puppies. If the threat continues, for example, if the person continues to move towards the dog or attempts to remove the puppies, the bitch may then bite. In extreme circumstances, if the perceived threat is too great for the bitch to cope with, she might even eat the toy or her puppies in an attempt to protect them.

Reducing maternal aggression

Bitches with maternal aggression are often not aggressive in other situations, and as the puppies grow she will become less protective of them. Often the best thing to do is to leave her and the puppies alone to avoid a conflict. Every time she becomes aggressive, the behaviour usually reinforces itself, because the bitch often succeeds in preventing the puppies from being removed. So the next time she perceives a threat to her puppies she may be more aggressive. You should never tease a bitch that has maternal aggression with toys or her pups.

To help to reduce the maternal aggression you should try to call the bitch away from her puppies. If she comes to you, you can praise her when she comes and sits for you in a calm, relaxed and non-aggressive way. This can help to ease her anxiety. If she is still interested in going for walks, use the opportunity to clean the whelping box and inspect and handle the puppies. You can also try to handle and inspect the puppies while the bitch is eating.

If the maternal aggression is associated with false pregnancy it is likely that it will happen again. For this reason, we recommend you consider having the dog desexed. This will prevent further false pregnancies and associated aggression.

Random aggression

People sometimes describe their dog's aggressive behaviour as being completely random. This is most likely because the early warning signs of another type of aggression were missed; truly random aggression is very rare. However, occasionally dogs can become aggressive when completely unprovoked.

As with many other types of aggression, random aggression most commonly first occurs at the onset of social maturity, at about 18 to 24 months of age, but can occur slightly earlier or later.

Random aggression is probably the most dangerous form of aggression, because it occurs without warning and can be very violent. In some cases people describe their dog attacking objects such as toys and the furniture. The dogs are often quite frantic, might salivate and have wide eyes with dilated pupils.

Reducing random aggression

It is important to remember that there may be a medical reason for any behaviour problem. Neurological conditions can sometimes trigger apparently completely random aggression. If you suspect that your dog has random aggression you should have your dog assessed by your veterinarian.

Dogs with truly random aggression can be dangerous and unfortunately there is no effective treatment. If you wish to attempt to manage a dog with random aggression, you should consult closely with a behaviourist, veterinarian or veterinary behaviourist. Sometimes medication can be tried, but does not succeed in all cases. If the dog does not respond to treatment, it is very difficult and dangerous to keep it as a family pet and, sadly, euthanasia may be the best option for your safety.

11:
Barking and vocalising

Vocalising is one of the major ways dogs communicate and is a normal part of canine behaviour (See Chapter two). However, excessive or inappropriate barking or other vocalisation can become a serious behaviour problem and a source of conflict between dog owners and their neighbours.

Barking and vocalising is an aspect of normal canine behaviour that has become exaggerated in domestic dogs, compared with wolves or dogs in the wild. You may have noticed that certain sounding barks are more common in some breeds than others. Terriers for example will bark with a high-pitched, yappy sound whereas Beagles or Basset Hounds often tend to howl. Staffordshire Bull Terriers can have a characteristic high-pitched cry or whimper. Dogs cannot speak the way people can, but they can use their 'voice' in other ways.

Many people notice that their dog has a different sounding bark in different circumstances. For example, when there is a visitor at the door, your dog may use the most threatening bark it can manage in order to warn the visitor. At other times, your dog might have a shorter, higher-pitched bark that it uses to attract your attention or when a toy is stuck behind the couch.

A dog might also bark when it is excited and anticipating going for a walk, riding in the car or greeting another dog. In the majority of cases, barking is completely normal. In fact, people rely on the fact that dogs bark; dogs would not be any good at protecting us if they could not alert the family to an intruder.

In most situations, you should be able to identify a reason for your dog's barking. There may have been a strange noise or a knock at the door for example. The dog might be barking to be let outside to go to the toilet or to initiate a game. Sometimes you may not be able to identify a reason for the barking.

There are two possible explanations for this. One explanation is that there is no reason at all for the barking and therefore the barking is abnormal and potentially a problem. Alternatively, there is actually a simple reason for the barking, but you just cannot identify it. You cannot hear many of the sounds dogs can. We know of a dog that lived near a hospital and could hear the ambulances before any people could, and he would mimic the sound of the siren by howling. Some dogs bark at sounds on the television or radio. Certain car sounds, like backfiring, will set some dogs off barking.

Most of the dogs that are labelled problem barkers are responding to their own environment and so are actually behaving normally. Some of these dogs, however, are not good at understanding the signals from the environment and are triggered to bark more easily than others. The aim of controlling problem barking is to teach these dogs to understand when it is appropriate to bark and when it is not.

Ideally, well-behaved dogs should not bark excessively when you are not there. Your dog should always look to you as the leader of the pack and therefore should stop barking as soon as you ask it to. Unfortunately, dogs like this are extremely rare. Usually the instinct or desire to bark is too great and despite the owner ordering the dog to stop, it does not do so immediately.

One of the most common barking problems we see is a dog that barks all day when its owner is away at work. Excessive barking causes neighbourly disputes, and if the problem is ongoing, the authorities may also become involved. Apart from this, it is also distressing for your dog.

So what causes a dog to bark all day or all night? Stress and anxiety, in particular separation anxiety, can a major cause. Some dogs bark excessively even when the owner is at home. Many people describe their dog's bark as being rhythmic, almost just a habit. The owner may be able to identify an initial trigger for the barking, but it may continue for much longer than is reasonable. Sometimes the pitch or tone of the bark changes, to a less controlled and more ritualistic bark. The dog might stare into space and appear to be just barking at the air.

It is often very difficult to stop the barking during one of these episodes, and this can be very frustrating and annoying. Many of the dogs which have this type of barking problem actually have a form of abnormal repetitive behaviour (see Chapter nine). Again, the underlying cause of this repetitive barking is most likely anxiety. If you are able to recognise a barking problem early and start to implement behaviour-modification techniques before the behaviour becomes too severe, you have a better chance of improving the problem.

Sometimes sickness or age can cause a dog to vocalise more than it used to. Older dogs, especially if they are losing their eyesight or hearing, tend to bark more. This is because they have to rely on vocalisation as a means of gaining information from the environment, because they no longer have accurate sight or hearing. Senility or Canine Cognitive Dysfunction is not an uncommon problem in older dogs and can cause the dog to bark at night or wander for no apparent reason. Other neurological conditions can cause this type of behaviour (see Chapter seven). You should take your dog to your veterinarian for a health check if it is developing changes in its behaviour.

Reducing your dog's barking

Most people expect a rapid solution to barking problems. Unfortunately there is no easy or rapid solution, and you need to be committed and patient with your dog. The barking will not improve unless you address the underlying problem. Anxiety is most likely the cause for excessive barking (see Chapter eight).

Do not encourage your dog to bark or 'speak.' This is especially true if your dog does not stop barking when you ask it to. Some highly trained dogs can be very entertaining and 'speak' on command. This is fine, because these trained dogs also stop speaking on command, and do not have underlying anxiety or barking problems.

You should not pick up your dog or try to calm it while it is barking, because this will send your dog the message that it is okay to bark and behave in this way. Your dog will associate its barking and excitable behaviour with your encouraging voice and be more likely to continue the barking in the future. Try to distract your dog as soon as it starts to bark using a sharp 'No!' Only once it has stopped barking and is calm should you speak soothingly and tell your dog it is okay and reward it with praise and treats.

To help to control problem barking, you need to teach your dog an appropriate alternative behaviour that it can perform instead of barking. An effective way to teach your dog when you are at home is to fit it with a head collar on a long lead. If you can reach the lead within 30 to 60 seconds after the barking starts, you can use the head collar and lead to gently close your dog's mouth. Combine this with ordering your dog to 'Sit'. Only once your dog is sitting in a calm and relaxed manner should you reward it with praise and a treat. During the training process it is useful to carry food rewards at all times. However, be careful because giving food or treats before the dog has stopped barking, or using food treats to distract it, can send the message to your dog that it will be rewarded for barking so this encourages the behaviour.

Barking is often a problem when you are not at home and you will not be able to implement these techniques when you are not around. You could consider using a citronella collar, which works by releasing a short, scented spray in response to the vibration of a dog's bark. It is not harmful for the dog and provides an immediate, unpleasant, but not painful, deterrent when the dog barks. You also know if your dog has been barking when you are out, because you will be able to smell the lemon scent of the citronella when you arrive home.

Most dogs learn that when the collar is on they cannot bark but as soon as it comes off, they may resume the barking ritual. For this reason a citronella collar should not be thought of as a quick fix, although it may help to keep your neighbours happy. For a more complete solution you need to implement other behaviour- modification techniques at the same time.

Electric shock collars are sometimes used for barking problems although they are not legally available in all areas. When the dog barks they deliver punishment swiftly and consistently, and the punishment does not persist significantly beyond the dog stopping the barking. However, unlike citronella collars the punishment is painful and can cause fear. If the cause of the barking is an underlying anxiety disorder, these collars have the potential to make the situation worse and they can even create an anxiety disorder. They should only be used under the advice of an animal behaviourist, veterinarian or veterinary behaviourist.

You need to practise with your dog every day to correct barking problems. It is time-consuming, but you can be successful by being committed and understanding what signals you are giving your dog (see Chapters two and five). You need to teach your dog that the best situation is for it to be calm. Pat your dog and praise it only when it is calm and relaxed of its own accord to reinforce the positive behaviour. Eventually, even when you are not at home, your dog will start to adopt this relaxed behaviour because it knows that this is what you, the pack leader, encourage.

12:
Destruction, digging and other common canine conundrums

D ogs can exhibit many potentially destructive or embarassing behaviours such as digging or mounting. In order to reduce such behaviours in your dog, you first need to understand why your dog behaves as it does. In this chapter we have addressed some of these issues.

Destructive behaviour

Dogs may become destructive for a variety of reasons. In order to stop the behaviour, you must first identify the underlying reason. Dogs can destroy many things, but the most common complaints are that the dog destroys items of clothing—often taken off the clothes line—as well shoes, furniture books and, of course, the garden.

Puppies are notorious for destructive behaviour, and this is mainly out of curiosity. Just like babies who are teething, puppies want to put everything in their mouths. They may not be able to chew on the bones you provide because they are too hard, but may find leather shoes very satisfactory as an alternative chew toy. It is important to provide puppies with regular training, socialisation with people and dogs, adequate exercise and appropriate chewing objects.

During the first six to twelve months of a puppy's life, you may need to 'puppy-proof' your home or at least those rooms that the puppy can access. This means packing away items it can potentially damage or objects with which it can damage itself. Electric power cords can be especially dangerous and should be concealed or covered with special protective sleeves. Some people use a crate or child-restraining area to contain the puppy in certain rooms. You should not keep the puppy in this area for long periods of time, and do not use it as a 'sin bin' where you banish the puppy when it is naughty. Although most puppies grow out of this behaviour, sometimes a puppy's tendency to chew various objects continues into adult life.

The most complicated cause for destructive behaviour is separation anxiety, and you need to address this in order to cure the problem (see Chapter eight). Providing your dog with a canine or feline companion does not usually help the problem if the underlying issue is anxiety.

Destructive behaviour can also be a form of attention-seeking behaviour. Even negative attention such as punishment will satisfy dogs that have an enormous need for attention. Unfortunately, destructive behaviour tends to damage the relationship between you and your dog. This makes it difficult to play with and praise your dog even when it is calm and relaxed, because you may be worried about stirring it up again. This means the dog does not receive any attention, even at appropriate times. This makes the destructive attention-seeking behaviour worse.

It is important not to yell at or actively push your dog away when it is seeking attention. Instead, if your dog jumps up for attention, passively let it fall off you by walking away or turning away. Any interaction at all, even pushing might be interpreted as positive reinforcement for the attention-seeking behaviour. If you cannot walk away or if your dog continues to jump up or bite at your clothing, you should banish it to a 'sin bin'. You should only give your dog attention and praise when it is calm and relaxed (see Attention-seeking behaviour on page 99).

You should praise your dog and give it attention when it is being good and behaving in a calm and relaxed way. It is easy to ignore a quiet dog, but if you do not reinforce the good behaviour, your dog will never learn what behaviour you expect or appreciate. You should also put some time aside daily to play with your dog. Play is a normal aspect of canine behaviour, but it should always be on your terms. You should be the one to initiate play and also to signal when it is time to stop. When your dog understands your signal that it is time to stop and is sitting quietly and calmly, you should praise it and pat it.

Puppies, young, active dogs and those that do not receive enough exercise or mental stimulation may turn to destructive behaviour in order to use up their excess energy. Some of these dogs will jump up at the owner all the time or steal objects people are using. This behaviour can be either to attract attention or is inappropriate play behaviour. When the dog constantly jumps up at its owner, the natural reaction is to push it down with or without a verbal correction. Even the act of pushing the dog may be interpreted by the dog as attention, and this might actually encourage the behaviour. Stealing can be particularly rewarding for a dog, because stealing typically results in a chase by the owner to retrieve the object, and this is a great game for the dog. This positive reinforcement encourages the stealing behaviour and the chewing that follows. Dogs that are deprived of play or have excess energy may seek out objects that are more interactive or appear to 'play back', for example dogs that shake pillows, unroll paper towels or toilet rolls and pull the washing off the line.

Do not punish your dog for being destructive hours after the event. Dogs cannot relate this to their behaviour if they are punished more than 30 to 60 seconds after the event. Punishing your dog hours later is not effective and will only make it scared of you or of the room in which it was punished. In some cases, this will actually make the behaviour worse because it exacerbates the dog's anxiety. Sometimes it may seem that the dog knows that it has done the wrong thing when you catch it because it cowers or is sheepish. The dog does not know that what it has done was wrong. It is cowering because it can sense your anger. Dogs do not hold resentment; your dog did not destroy the house in order to punish you.

It is critical that dogs with destructive behaviour receive enough exercise. It is not enough just to provide your dog with a large yard. You need to take it on a walk at least once a day. In the wild, the pack will walk together away from the den every day in search of food. Walking outside the home is important to keep your dog mentally stimulated and to give it an opportunity to socialise and spend its excess energy.

Provide your dog with appropriate objects it can chew, like indestructible toys. Hopefully, it will choose these over your shoes. Dog-proof or puppy-proof your house when you go out to avoid destructive episodes, or lock your dog in a room where the dog feels comfortable but cannot destroy anything when you are not there. If it is crate trained, you can leave it in the crate in a comfortable part of the house as long as the crate is large enough for the food and water, a comfortable bed and for the dog to turn around in.

Digging

Dogs dig holes for a number of reasons. Partly it is because they are naturally curious. Some dogs will scrape or dig at the ground after going to the toilet (see Chapter two). Another common reason is to bury something or uncover something, such as a bone or a toy. This is also a normal part of canine behaviour that has been encouraged in some breeds like jack russell terriers.

Some dogs have an incredibly strong desire to track scents and dig. You may never be able to teach these dogs not to dig. In these cases you need to provide your dog with a suitable place where it can dig without causing a problem.

For example, retrieval exercises used in some obedience classes can provide your dog with an alternative and more appropriate place to dig and an outlet for this behaviour.

Some dogs, especially puppies, amuse themselves by digging because it provides them with a game. It may be a challenge to try to uproot a plant. Obviously this must be great fun for the dog and acts to positively reinforce the digging behaviour. The only solution to this play behaviour is persistent supervision. As soon as the behaviour begins, you need to distract your dog and provide it with a more appropriate play thing. You also need to be aware that dogs that dig tend to be more active dogs and they need more active types of play than other dogs. Fetching a ball or Frisbee may provide a similar level of activity and stimulation without destroying the garden.

Occasionally dogs will dig holes for no reason at all. They do not sniff or paw at the ground, which is a normal component of tracking and hunting behaviour. They dig routinely and are very focused on the digging action. This type of behaviour may be a manifestation of abnormal repetitive behaviour (see Chapter nine), which will not respond to simple management strategies, so the underlying problem of anxiety needs to be addressed (see Chapter eight).

A less common reason for digging is that dogs sometimes use this as a way to find a warm or cool spot. The ground remains at a fairly constant temperature, so when the air is cold, your dog might dig a hole and crawl up into a tight ball within it to conserve heat. Similarly when the air is hot, the freshly unearthed dirt feels cool, and your dog may lie out flat in the hole and pant in an attempt to cool off. If this is the case, appropriate bedding or cool places should eliminate the digging problem.

You can reduce digging in pot plants by covering the dirt with chicken wire. If you catch your dog in the act of digging, you could use a long-range water pistol to startle the dog so it stops. This is not cruel to the dog and gives you an opportunity to ask the dog to perform another more appropriate behaviour you can praise such as play or sitting calmly.

Sometimes prevention is the only solution and you may need to invest in some fencing material to protect your lawn and potted plants!

Toileting problems

It is normal for puppies to urinate and pass stools in unusual locations while they are learning. Most puppies learn where they are allowed to go by about four to five months of age. They learn this most quickly if you praise the puppy when it goes in the right location and give it ample opportunities to do so (see The basics of housebreaking or toilet training on page 48).

If you catch your puppy or dog toileting inside, try to distract it and quickly take it to an appropriate location. Punishing the dog is only likely to make it frightened of you or of the particular part of the house and may create an anxiety problem. As with all behaviour problems, toileting issues are best identified and addressed early.

Despite correct housebreaking or toilet training, some dogs still go on to develop problems with toileting later in life. Depending on the cause, these problems can appear at any age. This can confuse many owners because the dog may have been house trained for several years.

There are several reasons why a dog may suddenly start to urinate or pass stools in a different or inappropriate location. In order to manage the problem, you first need to understand why the behaviour is occurring. To do this, you need to be patient and observant.

The first thing to do is to take your dog to see your veterinarian. There are many medical conditions that might cause your dog to urinate or pass stools inappropriately. Addressing the underlying condition should help to correct the behaviour problem as long as it is addressed in a timely fashion and the dog does not become accustomed to toileting in the house.

If you obtain an adult dog from a dog shelter, do not assume that it is already fully housebroken. The dog may go in the correct location most of the time but occasionally go inside the house. These dogs need to be re-trained in the same way that puppies are. Take the dog outside frequently, and praise it whenever it uses the correct location. You need to supervise it closely during the training time so you can actually be there to praise it. It can be harder to teach a dog to pass stools outside because there are generally less opportunities to praise the dog when they do this appropriately.

Some individual dogs have a preferred surface to use as a toilet. Some prefer to urinate on trees, others prefer grass and others are happy to go on hard surfaces such as concrete. This preference develops at about eight weeks of age. So you might have the opportunity to teach your young puppy which surface to use, but you may obtain the dog after it has developed a preferred surface. If there are no surfaces similar to its preference at its new home, it may try the carpet, or the wooden floors within the house as an alternative. In this situation, you need to start housebreaking again from scratch. Once again, this means taking the dog to the appropriate location frequently and rewarding it when it goes to the toilet there.

In some situations, a dog's needs change. For example, an older, arthritic dog may not be able to access the garden as easily as it used to because it is fearful and unsteady on the stairs. If a dog cannot access its usual toilet location, it will learn to use another more accessible location such as the carpet.

Anxiety is probably the most common behavioural cause of inappropriate urination. A dog may only have mild anxiety or anxiety only in certain situations but this can be enough to induce the dog to toilet in abnormal locations. Separation anxiety is the easiest type of anxiety problem to identify. These dogs will urinate in the house only when the owner is away or only when one particular person is away. Managing this problem involves addressing the underlying anxiety problem (see Chapter eight).

Dogs can become anxious or unsure in a number of other situations. Sometimes a change of routine or even a new visitor is enough for some dogs to become anxious. If the change of routine involves an addition to the household, such as a new baby, boyfriend or dog, then the natural hierarchy of the pack is disrupted. It will take a period of time before the dog finds its new place in the hierarchy. During this time, some dogs will toilet to mark their territory and to assert dominance. They may also do this because they are anxious. All new people should ask the dog to sit for treats and give attention to the dog only when it is calm and quiet. This sends a clear message to the dog that every person is above it in the pack hierarchy. Once the hierarchy is established the inappropriate toileting should stop.

Some dogs, especially young dogs, urinate when they are excited or when they are being submissive, but most dogs grow out of this. You can help to reduce this behaviour by ignoring the dog when it becomes excited. Encourage calm, relaxed behaviour, and walk away if the dog becomes overly excited. You should set some time aside every day to exercise your dog to allow it to spend some of its excited energy.

Extremely submissive dogs urinate when they are approached, reached over or sometimes in extreme cases even looked at (see Chapter two). It is difficult, but never comfort the dog when it appears submissive. Picking up, patting or comforting a dog when it is being submissive and urinating will only reinforce the behaviour and make it more likely to happen again. Dogs that urinate when they are submissive should be treated gently and calmly.

Never punish a dog that is being submissive, because this could make it fearful and make the submission and urination worse. Allow the dog outside to go to the toilet frequently to ensure that its bladder is always relatively empty during training sessions. You will need to use food rewards or play toys to teach a submissive dog not to urinate. When the dog sits and faces you, speak gently to it and offer it a reward. Only release the reward if it is not urinating. Also reward the dog, feed it and play with it only at times when it is not urinating. You need to practise these training techniques several times a day, but remember to try to keep the dog's bladder empty for each session to give it the best chance of success. You need to encourage confidence and independence by rewarding the dog at the right time when it is calm and relaxed and is not urinating inappropriately.

Roaming

All dogs have a desire to roam to some degree. It is normal for dogs to be curious and to want to investigate their environment. For some dogs this desire is stronger than for others. The desire to roam is the greatest in entire (undesexed) male dogs. This is because they are constantly seeking a mate. If there is a female dog on heat within the vicinity that the male dog can smell, the desire to roam becomes even greater. Dogs also have an increased desire to roam if they are not provided with adequate exercise or attention.

Roaming causes major problems within the neighbourhood, and it is unacceptable to allow our domestic pets to roam at their own free will. They are at risk of becoming injured or may attack other animals. We regularly see dogs that have been hit by a car while they were roaming. These accidents can be prevented if dogs are prevented from roaming.

To help reduce roaming, firstly you should have your dog neutered. This has its most significant effect if it occurs as a young puppy. If it is done after sexual maturity, at approximately six months of age, then some of the roaming behaviour will be learned. Neutering your dog will not always eliminate the problem entirely, but it will definitely help.

Provide your dog with sufficient exercise and attention. It has been suggested several times throughout this book, but it is worth repeating the fact that providing your dog with a yard is not a substitute for walking it. All dogs need leash walking at least once a day. Very active dogs will require more exercise than leash walking can give, and, if your dog is well trained, off-lead dog exercise areas are great because they allow your dog to run at its free will and spend more energy. It may also be a good idea to enrol in dog agility or obedience training to allow your dog to spend some of the excess energy it would otherwise use to roam.

Provide your dog with sufficient attention, mental stimulation and exercise. Dogs that do not receive enough attention may roam to seek it elsewhere or to spend their surplus energy.

Make sure that your yard is secure so that your dog cannot dig under, climb or destroy the fence in order to escape. It is amazing how clever and determined some dogs are. It is also important to make sure that your dog has adequate identification on its collar and is microchipped and registered so that if it does escape it can be identified and returned to you as quickly as possible.

Chasing cars, joggers and bikes

Dogs that chase joggers or bike riders can be frightening. You know your dog, and you may know that the fun may just be in the chase and that there is no aggression involved. However, the people at the receiving end of the chase do not know that yours is a friendly dog, and a rapidly approaching dog can be very threatening. This situation can easily escalate because the intimidated jogger or bike rider may threaten the approaching dog and therefore force the dog to become aggressive in response. This scenario is a disaster because the dog then learns to be aggressive to the people it chases. Dogs that chase cars risk being involved in or causing a road traffic accident.

There are two main reasons why a dog might chase cars, bikes, skateboard riders or roller bladers. The first and more common reason is that they are territorial. By default, they are usually successful in defending their territory, because the car or person just happens to be passing through. The dog thinks that it is succeeding in chasing the person away each time. This continual positive reinforcement means that the dog is encouraged to become a repeat offender, and it becomes very difficult to eliminate the behaviour. You may notice that when a dog chases a car, the dog becomes less interested as the car moves further away. This is not because the dog is tired, but because the car is leaving the dog's territory and the dog no longer needs to chase it out. These dogs can also have territorial aggression and pose a danger to anyone who approaches their territory (see Territorial or protective aggression on page 148).

The second reason that a dog might chase cars and people is that it is showing predatory behaviour. Dogs are predators by nature and in the wild they stalk and hunt to find their food. Most domesticated dogs no longer have a strong desire to hunt because they know that their pack or family will provide them with a regular meal. Some dogs, however, have retained the desire to stalk and pounce. You might notice that these dogs will hide behind an object as the car or bike is approaching and dart out at the last minute to grab the 'prey'. This is extremely dangerous behaviour because it can result in dog bite injuries. While most dogs do not actually bite, the threat of an approaching dog is frightening to people.

In order to reduce chasing behaviour in your dog, you need to provide your dog with all its simple needs in terms of exercise, mental stimulation and attention. One technique that you can try to reduce the behaviour is to leave your dog's lead on and ask a friend to pose as a jogger. As the dog gives chase, your friend can pick up the dog's lead and start jogging with it. This takes all of the fun out of the dog's chasing behaviour and can help to deter it from doing it. Sometimes the only way to stop dogs that chase cars, joggers and bikes is to keep them confined (see the previous section Roaming) or on a lead when they are in public.

Mounting and other embarrassing behaviours

There are two types of sexual behaviour that commonly cause embarrassment to dog owners and these are mounting and masturbation. Both entire (undesexed) and neutered dogs of both sexes mount, although it is more common in male dogs, especially when they are entire. Mounting can occur in a sexual or non-sexual context. Puppies, for example, use mounting during normal play to challenge another dog or to gain dominance. Mounting of people's legs is common, but is not usually related to sexual desire. In fact, mounting is more likely to be related to control and dominance. Mounting can also be an attention-seeking behaviour.

Mounting should never be encouraged. Occasional episodes should be discouraged with a sharp 'No!' and pushing the dog away. If the episodes are related to attention-seeking, however, you need to manage this by withholding all attention, passively walking away and allow the dog to slip off your leg. Do not actively push it away, because this will give the dog the attention that it wants. If the dog continues to mount you should banish it to a 'sin bin'. Only when it is being quiet, calm and relaxed should you then give it attention.

Both entire and neutered dogs of both sexes can masturbate. It may have been a learned behaviour that gave the dog pleasure in the past, or it may be a manifestation of an underlying anxiety problem. Neutered dogs may still be able to ejaculate, but this does not contain sperm so do not be alarmed if your neutered dog can ejaculate. Some dogs masturbate so frequently that it affects the way they interact with the family and other dogs. Again if this seems to be an attention-seeking behaviour, you need to address the underlying anxiety problem (see Attention seeking behaviour on page 99).

You should have your dog checked by your veterinarian for any health problems that may be contributing to the problem. Anti-anxiety medication may help to reduce the problem behaviour, and the dose may be able to be reduced or discontinued over time.

Rolling in unpleasant scents

Rolling is a part of normal canine behaviour and serves a few different functions. Firstly it is a way of marking one's territory. Rolling disturbs another animal's scent and replaces it with the dog's own scent. Secondly the act of rolling may be a self-grooming technique, as the friction on the ground helps to remove the dog's undercoat. The third reason is that, even though we as people might find the substance foul smelling, the dog may think it smells like perfume.

Unfortunately, many dogs love to roll in foul-smelling substances. The desire for dogs to do this can be very strong, and it can be a difficult behaviour to stop once it has started. It might help to bath the dog regularly and use a brush or comb to remove the old fur. Beyond this, the only solution is to keep your dog on a leash and within reach so you can physically stop it from rolling. If you cannot do this, or wish to allow your dog to have off-lead exercise, you will just have to accept that it is part of your dog's normal behaviour. Regular bathing can help to control any odours.

Car sickness

It is not uncommon for dogs to become sick in the car. This is either caused by motion sickness or because they are afraid of some aspect of travel. The fear may be of the moving car itself, traffic noise or leaving the house. Managing car sickness early and preferably during puppyhood will give you the best chance of success. Dogs that are afraid of the car, and all puppies, should be introduced to the car gradually. Puppies should be taken on short trips initially and encouraged and praised when they relax in the car. Take the puppy when it has an empty stomach. Initially you may notice drooling, vomiting or toileting. Be prepared, and use towels or blankets to protect the upholstery. Do not comfort your puppy if it becomes distressed. Comforting the dog at this time gives it the message that it is okay to be distressed and that you approve of this behaviour. Instead, you should distract the puppy by encouraging it to sit and relax. If it does relax or stops drooling, you can reward it by giving it a treat or a toy.

Adult dogs that are fearful of the car are more difficult to manage. You need to start slowly and be patient. Initially, sit the dog next to the car when it is not turned on. If it can relax and sit calmly, reward it with a treat. Next do the same but have the door of the car open. Each training session try to move the dog closer and closer to the car. Reward the dog every time it can sit and be calm around the car. You can also encourage the dog into the car as part of a game. If it is allowed to climb in and out of the car on its own terms, it will be much more relaxed. Start to have the dog sit in the car with the doors shut for increasing periods of time. Initially you should start with the windows open, but you can progress to having the car completely closed. Only praise the dog when it is relaxed and calm. Open the doors to let it out when it is calm.

You may need to practise each step several times a day for several days to proceed to the next step. It can take a long time to reduce a dog's fear of the car. When the dog can sit calmly in the car, you can start to feed it dinner or breakfast there. This makes the dog associate a positive experience with being in the car and also teaches it that nothing frightening happens when it is in the car.

When the dog is comfortable in the car when the engine is off, you can start the series of exercises with the engine running. Then you should take the dog for a short drive, just down the driveway, for example. Gradually you can increase the distance and speed you travel, as long as the dog remains calm and relaxed. If at any stage the dog becomes distressed, revert back to the previous step in the modification program and try again in a few days' time. As with any behaviour modification or desensitisation, accustoming a fearful dog to car travel can be time-consuming and requires patience, perseverance and consistency.

Index

A

abnormal repetitive behaviour, 108–21,
    159, 169
acral lick granuloma, 87, 117
aggression, 11, 45, 122–56
    dominance, 11, 48, 78, 132, 135–42
    fear, 46, 48, 78, 128–31
    food-related, 12, 47, 127, 131–5
    interdog, 82, 142–6
    maternal, 154
    play, 146–7
    prevention, 125–7
    protective, 148–53
    random, 155–6
    territorial, 148–53, 177
    visual signs, 22, 25, 26
alliances, 12
alpha dog, 13
anal glands, 33
anxiety, 91–107, 111–12, 159
    separation, 75, 93–9, 159, 165
    urination due to, 173
appetite, increased, 88
assertive behaviour, 22, 28
attention-seeking behaviour, 99–103, 110,
    120, 165–6, 178

B

barking, 31–2, 157–63
begging, 15
behaviour, 20–37
    abnormal repetitive, 108–21, 159, 169
    attention-seeking, 99–103, 110, 120,
        165–6, 178
    modifying, 15, 79, 103–7
    training, 64–80

bitches, 154–5
biting, 137
body language, 23
boredom, 111, 166
breed
    affect on communication, 35–7
    choosing, 39–42
    temperament, 42
breeding, 59, 92
bulldogs, 40
bull terriers, 117
buying a dog, 39–42

C

Canine Cognitive Dysfunction, 160
car sickness, 180–1
castration see desexing
Cavalier King Charles spaniels, 41, 42, 118
chasing cars and people, 176–8
chasing tail, 117
chewing, 115–18, 165
children and dogs, 138
choke chain, 66–8
choosing the right dog, 39–42, 125
citronella spray collars, 78, 162
cocker-spaniels, 41
collars, 66–8, 78, 116, 117, 139, 161–2
commands, 16–18, 51–5
communication, 20–37
    between dogs and humans, 31, 62
    visual, 21–5
conditioning, 69–70
costs of dog ownership, 39
counterconditioning, 75, 104, 106, 120, 152

D

dangerous behaviour, 156
defensive behaviour, 29–31
demanding attention, 17, 61
desensitisation, 74–5, 104, 106, 145
desexing, 19, 34, 56–8, 139, 175
destructive behaviour, 95–7, 164–78
digging, 168–70
discipline, 47
doberman pinschers, 117
dominance aggression, 11, 48, 78, 132,
        135–42
dominant behaviour, 13, 61

E

ear-clipping, 36
eating
    abnormal objects, 79, 112–15
    grass, 89–90
electric shock collars, 78, 162
Elizabethan collar, 116, 117
epilepsy, 118
euthanasia, 156
exercise, 39–40, 140
expenses, 39

F

facial expressions, 26
false pregnancy, 89
fear, 103–7, 128, 181
fear aggression, 46, 48, 78, 128–31
feeding, 15, 18
fleas, 115–16
food-related aggression, 12, 47, 127, 131–4

G

games, 141, 146–7
german shepherds, 117
golden retrievers, 117
grass, eating, 89–90
grooming, 40
growling, 25, 32

H

habituation, 73
health, 55–7, 86–9
housebreaking see toilet training
howling, 32
hunting, 83, 177

I

illness, 86–9, 112, 114, 160
    identifying, 62
inside dogs, 63
interdog aggression, 82, 142–6
introducing new pets, 83–5
itchy skin disease, 87

L

labrador retrievers, 117
leads, 66–8
licking, 20–1, 109, 115–19

M

maltese terriers, 39–40
mammary cancer, 57
masturbation, 179
maternal aggression, 154
medication
    anti-anxiety, 99, 103, 104, 107

anti-epileptic, 119
modifying behaviour, 15, 105–7
mounting, 29, 34, 178

N

neutering see desexing
neurological diseases, 89, 115, 118, 160
noise phobia, 74, 103

O

obesity, 39, 134
Old English sheepdogs, 37
omission training, 73
outside dogs, 63

P

pack structure, 10–19, 61, 152–3
    changes in rank, 12–14
pet insurance, 39
pets, introduction of other, 84
pica, 112–15
pit bull terriers, 42, 123
play, 141, 146–7, 166
play aggression, 146–7
playful behaviour, 27
pregnancy, 89, 154
prostatic hyperplasia, 57
protective aggression, 148–53
pugs, 35, 40
pullis, 37
punishment, 76–8, 95, 167
puppies, 28, 38–59
    choosing, 43–4
    destructive behaviour, 164–5
    developmental periods, 45–6
    discipline, 47

health and maintenance, 55–7
learning pack position, 11, 45
socialisation, 46
toilet training, 48–50
training, 51–5
vaccination, 46
pyometra, 57

R

rank, 12–14, 135–42
rank reduction program, 15–19, 140, 145–6
repetitive behaviour see abnormal repetitive
    behaviour
rewards, 52, 71–2
Rhodesian ridgeback, 37
roaming, 174–6
rolling in unpleasant scents, 179–80
routine, 121

S

schnauzers, 40, 41
self-mutilation, 115–19
separation anxiety, 75, 93–9, 159, 165
shaping, 69
shar peis, 41
sickness see illness
sitting, 17
skin diseases, 87, 115
sleeping, 15, 18, 63
smell, sense of, 33
snapping at air, 118
social interaction, 35, 46
stealing behaviour, 167
stereotypic behaviour see abnormal repetitive
    behaviour
submissive behaviour, 22, 174
subordinate dog, 11

T

tail-docking, 36
tail position, 23, 25
territorial aggression, 148–53, 177
thirst, increased, 87–8
thunderstorms, fear of, 74, 103–5
training, 17, 51–5, 65, 68–80, 126
    avoidance, 79
    conditioning, 69–70
    counterconditioning, 75, 104, 106, 120, 152
    desensitisation, 74–5, 104, 106, 145
    extinction, 73
    flooding, 76, 104
    omission training, 73
    positive reinforcement, 64, 69–70
    punishment, 76–8
    rewards, 52, 71–2
    shaping, 69
    vocalisation in, 32–3
    with other dogs, 81–2
toilet training, 48–50, 170–1
toileting problems, 170–4

U

urination, 28, 29, 34, 49–50, 86, 173
urine marking, 29, 33–4
uterus infection, 57

V

vaccination, 46
veterinarians, 56
    reducing dogs' fear of, 106
visual cues and signals, 21–3
vision, 21
    impaired, 27
vocalisation, 20, 31–2, 157–63

W

wagging tail, 25
waiting for commands, 17–18
wolves, 35, 36

Y

yelping, 32

Further Reading

Milan C and Peltier M J, *Cesar's Way: The Natural, Everyday Guide to Understanding and Correcting Common Dog Problems,* Three Rivers Press 2007.

Milan, C and Peltier M J, *Be the Pack Leader: Use Cesar's Way to Transform Your Dog ... and Your Life,* Harmony 2007.

Benjaminm C L, *The Chosen Puppy: How to Select and Raise a Great Puppy from an Animal Shelter*, Howell Book House, 1990.

Fogle B, *The Dog's Mind: Understanding Your Dog's Behaviour*, Howell Book House 1990.

Weston D and Ross R, *Dog Problems: The Gentle Modern Cure*, Howell Book House 1990.

Weston D and Ross R, *Dog Training: The Gentle Modern Method*, Howell Book House 1990.

Richardson J and Cole L S, *The Dog Whisperer*, New Holland Publishers 2001.

Fogle B, *Know Your Dog: An Owner's Guide to Dog Behaviour*, Howell Book House 1992.

Weston D and Ross R, *Second-Hand Dog: How to Turn Yours Into a First-Rate Pet*, Howell Book House 1988.

Fox M W, *Superdog: Raising the Perfect Canine Companion,* Howell Book House 1996.

Benjaminm C L, *Surviving Your Dog's Adolescence: A Positive Training Program*, Howell Book House 1993.

By the same author

FIRST AID FOR CATS

Recognising common ailments and accidents

Dr Justin Wimpole BVSc

FIRST AID FOR DOGS

What to do before you take your sick dog to the Vet

About the authors

Both Justin and Kate knew they wanted to be veterinarians when they were young children. They met while studying Veterinary Science at the University of Sydney. Both have also spent time studying and researching at the College of Veterinary Medicine at Cornell University in the United States. After graduating they embarked on careers in small animal practice.

Justin is currently the Senior Registrar in Small Animal Medicine at the Small Animal Specialist Hospital, Sydney, while Kate is pursuing a doctorate in medical research, studying ovarian cancer in humans. She still practises as a veterinarian and hopes some of the skills and knowledge that she is learning in medical research will translate back to the veterinary world and help her four-legged patients.

Justin has previously authored the bestsellers *First Aid for Dogs* and *First Aid for Cats*, both published by New Holland Publishers. Kate is a capable artist and provided the illustrations for *First Aid for Cats* as well as *Canine Communication*.

Together they own a beautiful boxer named Milo, who is a renowned canine blood donor. His donations have saved over a dozen dogs' lives. They also own a black-and-white cat named Beetle, who is just fantastic, if sometimes a little cheeky. Beetle and Milo get on famously, but Beetle is definitely the boss. These two provide Justin and Kate with endless enjoyment and inspiration for their work.

Notes on your dog's behaviour and health

Date   Comments

. . . .

. . . .

. . . .

. . . .

. . . .

. . . .

. . . .

. . . .

. . . .

. . . .

. . . .

. . . .

Date	Comments
....	....
....	....
....	....
....	....
....	....
....	....
....	....
....	....
....	....
....	....
....	....
....	....
....	....
....	....

Notes

Date   Comments

. . . .

. . . .

. . . .

. . . .

. . . .

. . . .

. . . .

. . . .

. . . .

. . . .

. . . .

. . . .

. . . .

. . . .